SEO
SIMPLIFIED

FOR SHORT ATTENTION SPANS

Learn the Essentials of
Search Engine Optimization
in Under an Hour

BARRY FELDMAN

Featuring contributions from SEO experts
Andy Crestodina, Brian Dean and
Jayson DeMers

SEO Simplified for Short Attention Spans

Copyright © 2015 Barry Feldman

First Edition

ISBN-13: 978-1518822209

www.feldmancreative.com/books

TABLE OF CONTENTS

INTRODUCTION

SEO ISN'T SUCH A HAIRY BEAST

"You're not optimizing your site for search," my client said between bites of his burger. "You're shooting yourself in the foot, man. How's anyone going to find it?"

I knew he was right. I knew just enough about the subject of SEO to know I didn't know diddley-squat. To me the practice of search engine optimization seemed like such a massive hairy beast, so I conveniently avoided it.

I wanted to believe my writing chops would suffice. He assured me in a marketing era now dominated by the web, they wouldn't. He spoke the truth.

He went on with the lesson telling me I really didn't need to become an expert in SEO and with a basic understanding of what to do, I'd benefit in a huge way. I know now, he was right about that too.

But I'm not the type who typically just scratches the surface of a topic I've taken an interest in. I always feel the need to become a subject matter expert. So I decided to buy a few highly regarded books about SEO.

I dug in. Actually, it'd be more accurate to say I tried. The books were nasty long technical volumes that confused the crap out of me. I filed those books away on the shelf not having finished either.

I'm not a professional SEO. (Search engine optimization professionals like to call themselves that.) I've never taken a course on the topic.

And I never will. Why? I get it now.

I suspect you don't want to read thick books on SEO or commit a lot of your time and money attending SEO school. You don't need to.

SEO is not the hairy beast I thought it was. I know enough to share with you what truly matters: how to get your key web pages ranked on the first page of search to generate traffic from people that are actually qualified to buy what you sell.

This short book will give you the foundation you need to get your head around SEO, get started and get ranked.

I've been a copywriter for more than 25 years. I've been a content strategist, blogger and content writer for just a few. The conversation I told you about took place years ago when I had just started blogging on my first WordPress website. I'm grateful it happened.

The blog posts and pages I write now don't take up an insignificant place in cyberspace. Many rank on the first page of search for highly searched-for keywords, several in the top spot. They're conceived, written and optimized to appear when some stranger has questions I'm qualified to answer. They serve as magnets to my website attracting people that are interested in learning from me and investing in the services I offer.

If you're a content marketer and want to save time in your quest to understand and apply the essential principles of SEO, this book is for you. Much of the content comes from blog posts I've written about SEO that are top dogs on search.

Three invaluable bonus lessons come to you courtesy of a trio of giant experts on the subject of search: Brian Dean of Backlinko, Andy Crestodina of Orbit Media Studios, and Jayson DeMers of AudienceBloom.

Brian gave me permission to share his SEO copywriting secrets with you. Andy joined me for an interview where we spent 30 minutes uncovering precisely how he gets ranked on page one of search results for about half of the content he creates. Jayson agreed to have me share his list of reasons why you may not be ranking on search.

It'll take you less than an hour to soak up the lessons I've learned and validated the past four years.

Despite the dizzying array of channels that have emerged in digital marketing, search remains the biggest driver of traffic. A stunning majority of clicks from search results come from the listings on page one.

Let's get you there.

CHAPTER 1

WHY IS SEO IMPORTANT?

SEO is the digital God, the almighty power of the Internet. It has been ever since Google seized control. We put our faith in it to help solve the challenges of our daily lives.

The search engine doesn't come to us. Many forms of marketing do. Or at least they try to. They interrupt us. We generally make them go away. Or we go away. Or we simply ignore them.

Search is kind and sensitive. We summon it in our time of need. When we:

- Want to learn
- Want to buy
- Want to be entertained

Search won't let you down.

Search brings you buyers

The majority of web traffic is generated by search. Your visitors arrive by choice.

As much as you might perfect your other digital initiatives, search marketing is likely to generate higher conversion rates.

See, visitors from search have intent. They are looking for something.

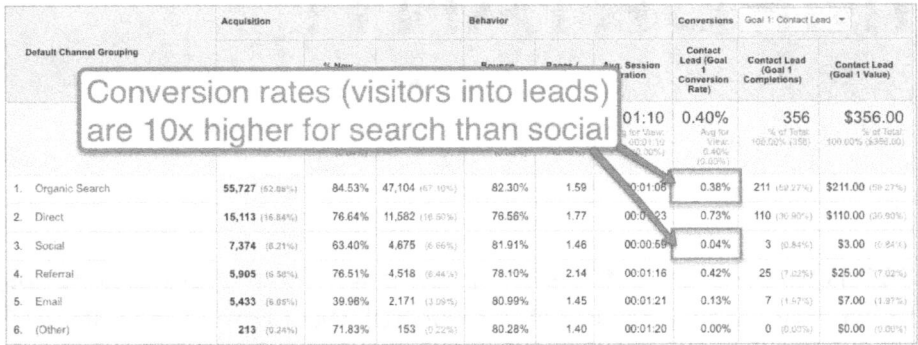

My friend Andy Crestodina, author of Content Chemistry,[1] helped me make this point. When he compares conversion for search vs. social the evidence proves search converts by a factor of 10 over social.

SEO should represent you well

The Internet is a free-for-all. You can't control what's written about you, be it true or false. Kind or harmful.

With the power of SEO working for you, you can help readers understand your intentions. You can serve them messages that cast you in the best light.

You can be relevant. Helpful. Interesting. These are tenets of search marketing.

Search makes you a smarter marketer

SEO planning requires you to do keyword analysis, which is essentially market research. You'll make discoveries about the size of your market and the strengths and weaknesses of your competition.

With some analysis and deductive reasoning you'll come to learn more about your customers too:

- How they search
- How they navigate your site
- The language they use
- The technology they use
- The region they live in
- When they're most active

Google gives you the gift of analytics. Much of the data you capture isn't served on a silver platter. It may not answer every question you have. But there's no question, your analytics delivers the intel you need to make smarter marketing decisions.

SEO is kind

Search engines are easy to get to. They're easy to use. If you don't want to type to them, you're welcome to talk. You can hop from device to device as you wish. Search remains ready and waiting on standby for the touch of your hand.

SEO makes friends easily too. Social media, branding and other marketing strategies complement SEO and vice-versa. They work together to forward your cause.

Sometimes marketers feel the need to compare marketing tactics. They choose some and leave others out. SEO discourages such nonsense. It longs to be a part of your plan.

Search extends your hours

Your successful SEO efforts drive prospects to your open-all-night-and-weekends-too place of business.

SEO builds credibility

Appearing high—and often—on search results builds your brand. Topping a SERP is bound to have a psychological effect on the searcher. Your ranking is a vote of confidence.

"Look at that. This company must lead the field."

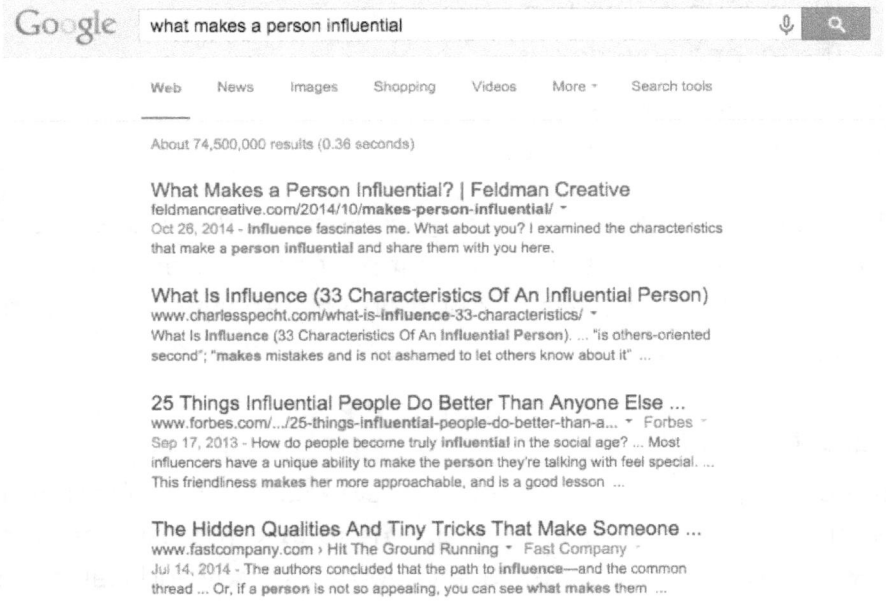

Number one? Outranking Forbes and FastCompany? Little old me? With SEO knowledge comes marketing power. I wrote this content with a long tail search strategy in mind and it became a leading traffic generator for my website.

SEO is measurable

Every element of your SEO can be measured, analyzed and ultimately refined. The more committed you are to the process, the more you'll gain from it.

SEO is marketing

"Your search strategy is your business strategy," wrote Vanessa Fox in her book, *Marketing in the Age of Google*.[2] I read that a few years back and it's stuck with me.

SEO truly is a core marketing activity. It must be tied to your business goals. Succeeding with search forces you to carefully examine what your message is and whom it's for.

SEO is cost-effective

SEO can be a highly cost-effective form of marketing. In fact, you can get into it and make progress with a modest degree of know-how and free tools.

Will you benefit from bringing in experts and employing some power tools? Sure. If your business is complex and highly competitive or you have a massive website, or multiple websites, you should consider enlisting help. Still, it's simply time you're paying for.

An expert consultant may help bring more focus to your business. You may find it wise to steer clear of markets that are too small or competition that's insurmountable. The investment could pay for itself with this alone because you'll avoid investing time where you shouldn't and focus on getting potentially higher-converting traffic.

Guesswork is expensive. A solid SEO strategy can be golden.

SEO has staying power

Yes, search evolves perpetually. Yes, you can be on top today and invisible tomorrow. Yes, your competition covets the place you earned on page one of a search result.

But the truth is, search is a big, slow boat. Given some time, it may turn, but it's not susceptible to the minor breezes that blow.

Another truth is search engines are unfathomably smart. Tricksters don't fool it.

Cheaters pay the price. So a final truth is you have to earn a spot on page one of a search engine results page (SERP). When you do, you can reap rewards for a long time.

As far as I can tell, every other online marketing play has a far more fleeting effect.

If you don't rank, your competitors will

Potential buyers are sure to search for answers to their questions. They're going to find them. Will those answers be yours or your competitor's?

When you lose at search, you lose sales. Please say it with me. "When you lose at search, you lose sales."

Amen. And praise Google.

CHAPTER 2
SEO SIMPLIFIED

"We really do want to understand SEO."

I was on a conference call with a client who said that. And then:

"Let's plan to have a 15 minute call where you can explain SEO to us."

Gulp. Can SEO really be simplified to that extreme? Perhaps the basics can. That's what I had in mind when I set out to write what you're about to read: SEO, with a spoonful of sugar.

What's SEO mean?

Search engine optimization. It's a clunky term for sure. You can't optimize search engines. In fact, you can't even learn exactly how they work. These are well-guarded secrets.

What can you do? You can do the right thing to your website's pages—*optimize them*—to increase the likelihood Google and the other search engines know where they are and what they contain, so it will present them as a recommended resource when they match a search.

That's not all you can do. It's ground zero—what you have to do. And though you need to understand what you're up against to do it well, this activity, defined as "on-site optimization," is the easy part.

The other stuff you can do represents the hard, but more meaningful part. This other stuff happens "off-site." I'm going to explain.

But for now, to answer the question, I'll say SEO means *the things you do on-site and off to help get presented by a search engine and discovered by its users.*

Search engine rankings are largely based on popularity

Essentially, people turn to a search engine because they have a question. The search engine's job is to offer a directory of potential answers.

To help you find the answer you seek, the search engine tries to calculate the relevancy of web pages. The more relevant the page, the higher it will rank in the results.

> SEO boils down to indicating the relevance of your content to the search engines.

To determine relevance, search engines use algorithms, complicated mathematical formulas written (and perpetually refined) to robotically determine what content is worthy of being presented in response to a search.

How's it do this? Everyone would like to know the answer, but no one actually does. So they speculate. Test. Measure. And they attempt to tell, or sell, you highly informed theories.

But at a broad level, most can agree search engines base rankings on:

- The quality of the content and
- The popularity of the content (which is assumed to reflect the prior)

For a very long time, because it was possible to convince the search engine your site and its pages were relevant through the careful execution of sleazy and unethical tactics, a great big sleazy and unethical business exploded. It was called SEO. Today, a great many SEO companies purposely steer the conversation in the direction of content marketing, a much less controversial subject.

Why? Because content is the one thing that holds steady in search.

Understand basic on-site and on-page signals

If you're going to have a fighting chance to rank you need to abide by some ground rules. Essentially, you must set up your web pages such that they contain the basic elements search engines are capable of discovering.

You see, your website is "crawled" by "spiders." That's the metaphor, like it or not. The spiders seek out words—keywords—to create an index of the content offered on your pages.

> Your challenge is to understand the proper places
> to put the keywords so the search engine understands
> the page's content.

Title tag— You title (and at the code level, "tag") each page to tell the search engines what the page is about. Again, you do this with keywords. You need to choose them carefully and use them naturally. You also should limit your titles to 60 characters (or so) so they are presented in their entirety.

Your title tag (and all the tags we'll review) belongs in a specific field in your HTML code. HTML is the language browsers and search engines understand. It may sound intimidating, but with some very basic training on using your content management system (CMS), you'll understand exactly where to put each tag (and also get guidance regarding the appropriate length).

Keywords in the copy—Throughout the copy on your page, you'll want to use keywords and variations of them. Do not overuse keywords for the sake of SEO. (Keyword stuffing can result in damaging penalties by search engines.) However, consider these smart keyword placement tactics, which help to optimize your page:

- Use keywords near the beginning of the page's copy.
- Use keywords and practical variations in your subheads. You'll tag subheads with H2 and H3 designations in your HTML (H means "header").
- Search engines are unable to "read" images, so when placing an image, take advantage of the "alt text" tag by giving the image a name, which includes a keyword.
- Use keywords once in the URL whenever possible.

Meta description—Meta descriptions provide concise explanations of the contents of web pages.

Meta descriptions are often misunderstood. They are *not* a part of the page optimization equation. Still, they should be taken seriously because they affect the user's decision to click or not. See, the search engine will often present the meta description you provide as the copy snippet displayed in your listing.

Meta Description Tag - Learn SEO - Moz
https://moz.com/learn/seo/**meta-description** ▾ Moz ▾
Meta descriptions are HTML attributes that provide concise explanations of the contents of web pages. **Meta descriptions** are commonly used on search engine result pages (SERPs) to display preview snippets for a given page.

The meta description above helps the reader understand the page's content. The keywords used are bolded in the snippet. Meta descriptions are limited to 160 characters.

URLs—Your page's URL should contain your keywords, but be as concise as possible. URLs are automatically generated (in many CMSs) based on the page title, so edit them to remove unnecessary words. Words in a URL should be separated by hyphens.

Internal links—Search engines aim to understand the structure of your site. It's useful to create links within your copy to other pages on your site. Using this practice may also serve to help your readers discover additional content and therefore increase time spent on your site and have a better learning experience.

That's it for on-page optimization. There's no need to overthink or overdo it.

The keys to keyword selection

Though search engines are immensely powerful, they're unable to read minds. Searchers must type or speak to the search engine. Basically, as a user, you feed the search engine words. In SEO, these are referred to as "keywords."

> Choosing keywords for your content is a critical first step in SEO.

It's important to recognize doing keyword research and selection effectively not only generates traffic to your site, *it delivers the right kind of traffic—prospective buyers.*

The smart money is on keywords

SEO only works when you select keywords for which you can achieve high rankings. But it's not as simple as defining the obvious categories that describe your business. In addition to the relevance of your keywords, you need to consider:

1. *Search volume*—The number of people who search for the phrase in the geographic area you serve
2. *Competition*—The websites already ranking for the phrase

Assessing search volume is the easier part of the formula. Even if you don't intend to invest in Google's pay-per-click program, AdWords, you can open a free account and begin using the Google Keywords Planner.

- On the start page, select "Search for new keywords" under "Find new keywords and get search volume data."
- Enter one or more keywords (meaning single words or phrases).

- In the "Keyword ideas" tab you'll be shown the average number of searches for the *exact* keyword.

- The estimated numbers are based on the date range, location, and targeting settings you select.

- Round numbers are shown, which can be as low as 10.

- While 10 may appear to be a small number, it's conceivable no number is insignificant for beginning your SEO efforts.

- Below the keywords you searched will be up to 800 additional ideas sorted from most to least relevant according to Google's data. Search volume data is presented for each.

Assessing competition isn't nearly as easy. While the keywords planner reveals generalized competitive ratings (low, medium, or high), you don't want to apply them. The data is meant to inform pay-per-click decisions.

The tool you do want to rely on here is MozBar, a free extension installed in your Chrome or Firefox tool bar. You'll use MozBar with Google search along with some intuition.

- Toggle your MozBar to the on position. A capital M shows white-on-blue.

- Do a Google search for the keyword you're considering.

- A MozBar appears beneath each organic search result revealing scores for three data points: PA, links, and DA.

- PA is "page authority," an estimation by Moz reflecting their prediction of how well the page will rank on search engines.

- Links reveals the inbound links (from sites other than your own).

- DA is "domain authority," an estimation of how well the website (not individual page) will rank on search engines.

The numbers provided by MozBar should help you consider the competitive field for the keyword you searched, particularly the DA. Much further insights will be provided on how to assess your competition in the first bonus chapter of this book, *How to Get Your Blog Post on the First Page of Google.*

For now, just understand Moz scores should be evaluated relative to the DA of your website. The general idea, strategically speaking, is to settle on keywords where some of the top ten DAs reported are in the range of your own—or below it. A page full of DA scores well above yours suggests it will be highly difficult to rank for the keyword you're investigating.

When you begin doing keyword research, you'll very quickly learn the short simple keywords you covet (usually one or two-word phrases) are impossibly competitive. The more competition you have, the less likely you'll appear on the first page of a search engine results page (SERP). And, the reality is, the first page is the only page that matters because it earns an overwhelming majority of the clicks.

All hope is not lost. If you shift your strategy to long tail keywords—phrases of three or more words—you can find opportunities to rank on the first page and likely drive more qualified prospects to your web pages.

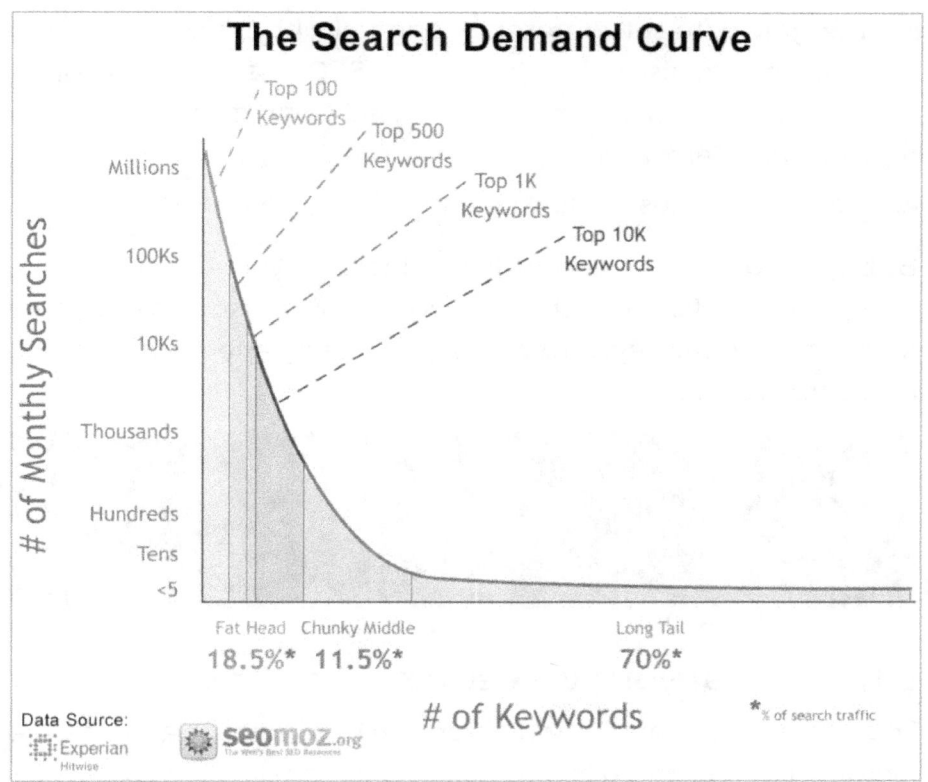

This chart depicts the long tail strategy.

- The y-axis shows search volume.

- The x-axis is the number of words in the search string (or keyword phrase).

- As the number of words in the search increase, the volume of search decreases.

- On the left side, searches for top keywords are searched in the millions, 100Ks, etc. These terms, commonly called "head" terms, are likely to be single words, e.g. SEO, baseball, convertible.

- The search volume decreases into the 100s in the "chunky middle," where phrases are 2 or 3 words, e.g. SEO lessons, baseball stadiums, used convertible.

■ The gray data set represents long tail phrases where search volume is measured in the 10s, e.g. SEO lessons for websites, baseball stadiums with domes, used Corvette convertible in Northern California.

■ 70% of searches are for the long tail keyword phrases.

By targeting long tail keywords, you increase your chance to succeed as a "big fish in a small pond." If you pursue the strategy for many long tail keyword phrases, you can generate significant traffic from search.

> If your company does not operate a well-established, high traffic website with high authority, long tail keywords are the secret to your success with search.

Links reveal your website's popularity

Though it's commonly understood 200 or more variables are factors in determining the search engine ranking of a web page, the most important one is link popularity.

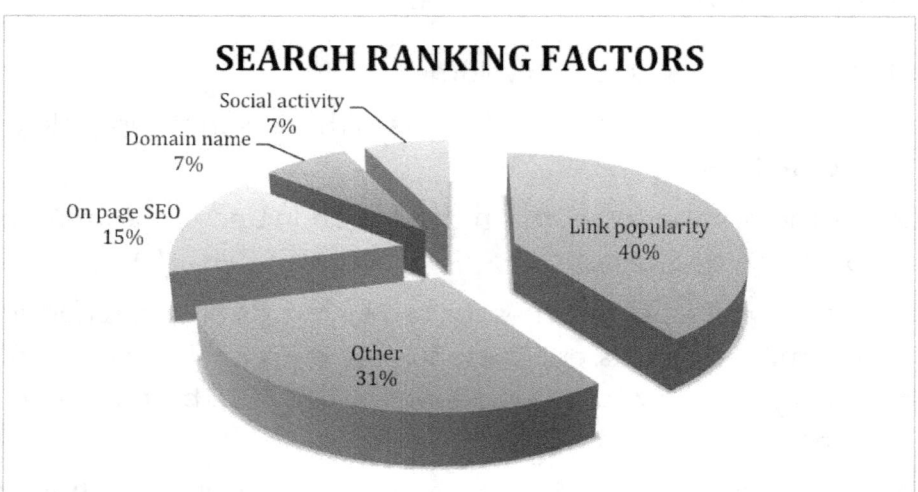

Source: Content Chemistry, An Illustrated Handbook for Content Marketing by Andy Crestodina

- **Link popularity** is based on the number of links from other websites to your page and also considers the authority or rank of the websites containing the links. The most trusted websites tend to link to other trusted websites.

- **Other factors** include metrics such as page load time, click through rates from search engines, search volume for the company, and the freshness of the content.

- **On-page SEO** is mostly attributed to the use and placement of keywords.

- **Domain name** refers to the use of keywords in your URL.

- **Social activity** is a hotly debated factor, but SEO professionals generally agree social activity applies (or at least correlates). Most say social signals from Google+ loom largest.

Andy Crestodina, a recognized expert from Orbit Media, explains, "It's clear that links on other people's websites are a big factor in how high you rank in search engines. If you're serious about SEO, getting good links has to be a part of your content marketing efforts."

After keyword research, link building is the next most important SEO activity. The most commonly useful and acceptable strategies to earn links (leading to higher relevance and ranking) include:

- **Blogging**—An informative and entertaining business blog is the most valuable SEO practice. The company can control what it publishes. Successful blogs not only populate the website with keyword-based content, but earn links from other blogs and websites.

- **Great content**—Well-received content beyond blog posts has "link bait" potential. That is, it can earn links and social sharing (which may also earn links).

- **News**—Earning the attention of news media tends to result in links.
- **Partnerships**—Partners, customers and employees often act as advocates and express their appreciation for your company and its content through links.

Three must-have SEO tools

There are countless tools, free and paid, you can use to practice search engine optimization. Three free must-have tools for beginners and experts alike are:

- Google AdWords Keyword Planner—The tool helps you build search strategies by supplying keyword data and ideas. (https://adwords.google.com/KeywordPlanner)
- Open Site Explorer by Moz—The tool tracks your website's link profile against competitors, identifies top pages, shows social activity data and provides other useful analytics. (https://moz.com/researchtools/ose/)
- MozBar—The tool is toggled off and on with your Chrome or Firefox browser. As you search and surf, MozBar presents SEO metrics (including page authority and domain authority), which will help determine how difficult it is to rank for specific keywords. (https://moz.com/tools/seo-toolbar)

Focus on content

I hope you were able to get your head around the basics of SEO and the tactics used to increase your search engine rankings. You now need to get to work. As a content marketer, you must focus on publishing valuable content because there is no more powerful SEO strategy for success.

CHAPTER 3

SEIZE AN ADVANTAGE WITH THE RIGHT KEYWORDS

Winning at SEO calls for outmaneuvering the field.

Let's examine how to find keywords your competitors aren't using—with tactics they don't even know about.

"Keywords don't matter much anymore." You find it written everywhere lately.

I asked a friend who eats analytics for breakfast and snacks on SEO all day long, "Whatcha' think about that, man?" He smirked. Then he turned toward his massive monitor, typed "g-o-o-g-l-e-(.)-c-o-m" on his keyboard. The ubiquitous page with the crude, but familiar multi-color logo and single blank field popped right up.

He turned back to me and said, "What do I do now, Barry?" His point was pretty clear. However all-powerful the search engine that changed the world may be, it can't yet read your mind. Whether you choose to type or talk, you tell it what you're looking for with a string of words.

Notice I wrote, "string of words." I meant to suggest three, four, or more, words. As I wrote in the previous chapter, these searches are known as "long tail" and represent the majority of searches. It's also important to note long tail keywords, being more specific than one or two word searches, have proven to deliver superior conversion.

To illustrate, consider "acoustic guitar" vs. "Used Taylor 12-string acoustic-electric guitar." It seems intuitive the longer, far more specific term suggests the searcher has a better idea of the product he seeks and is therefore closer to reaching for his wallet. Research consistently provides confirmation.

Perhaps an even more important reason long tail keywords enter the SEO discussion so often is because as an online marketer you have a remarkably higher chance of earning page one search results by developing content targeting the lengthier phrases. And again, the "big fish in a small pond" metaphor applies.

By strategically implementing long tail keywords, you're far more likely to rank high, attract the audience you desire, and show motivated prospects the way to your website.

Your challenge is to identify the right long tail keywords

How do you do this?

Almost anyone you ask will immediately cite Google Keyword Planner, a tool made available for free to anyone who registers for an account. As advertised, Keyword Planner will provide keyword ideas and traffic estimates. However, it's a safe bet to assume your competition will be using the very same tool, get served the same data, and are likely to make similar decisions.

Consider the advantage you'll seize if you're able to identify untapped long tail keywords the competitors in your niche don't know about or use.

The roads less traveled

Understand, Google Keyword Planner isn't all that great about delivering *new* keyword ideas. The keywords you're shown are of course tied to the term you enter and that's that. However, if you want to explore the roads less traveled by competitors, it's time to try alternative and smart ways to find niche keywords.

According to *Keyword Research: The Definitive Guide*[3] by Backlinko, your goal is to identify niche markets, subsegments of larger markets. The eBook explains you begin by creating a niche cloud map. You create "clouds" that float around your industry.

Backlinko offers the following example:

At the center, the main cloud is the product: *basketball hoops.* The clouds surrounding it could include:

- Free throw shooting
- Basketball highlights
- Vertical jumps
- Sports nutrition
- Dribbling technique
- Basketball shoes

These are merely examples. The list could go on, and with each cloud, or tangent, you might discover more niches and opportunities. That's the basic idea.

Maybe this cloud floating (or mind mapping) type of exercise will come easy to you. Maybe it won't. The good news is there are quite a few useful hack-like approaches that will serve you well. And in fact, while niche hunting, you'll find you're conducting market research and getting inside the minds of your customers.

Start with Wikipedia

Maybe you curse Wikipedia for dominating page one Google results the way it does, but check this out. I entered "antivirus software" in Wikipedia.

The table of contents shows a plethora of related terms the Keyword Planner is unlikely to: "signature-based detection," "rogue security applications," "hardware and network firewall." These could be niche keywords worth considering.

And that's just the table of contents. The long and detailed article on the topic introduces hundreds of related terms, most of them linked to additional resources. For instance,

Contents [hide]

1 History
    1.1 1949-1980 period (pre-antivirus days)
    1.2 1980-1990 period (early days)
    1.3 1990-2000 period (boom of the antivirus industry)
    1.4 2000-2005 period
    1.5 2005 to present
2 Identification methods
    2.1 Signature-based detection
    2.2 Heuristics
    2.3 Rootkit detection
    2.4 Real-time protection
3 Issues of concern
    3.1 Unexpected renewal costs
    3.2 Rogue security applications
    3.3 Problems caused by false positives
    3.4 System and interoperability related issues
    3.5 Effectiveness
    3.6 New viruses
    3.7 Rootkits
    3.8 Damaged files
    3.9 Firmware issues
4 Performances and other drawbacks
5 Alternative solutions
    5.1 Hardware and network Firewall
    5.2 Cloud antivirus
    5.3 Online scanning
    5.4 Specialist tools
6 Usage and risks
7 See also
8 References
9 Bibliography
10 External links

I clicked "intrusion detection systems" and related ideas came flying at me.

Find common questions on forums

When your goal is to crawl inside the mind of customers and gain insights into topics being discussed in your niche, snooping around in industry forums can be enormously informative.

I did a search for "digital printing +forums" and selected the first listing, "Digital Printing Discussion – Print Planet." Bingo. The forum site presented 408 threads.

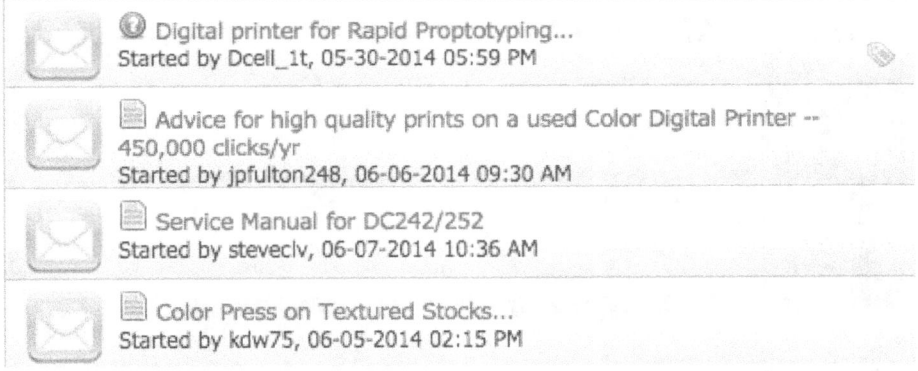

I'd consider the titles (or at least, ideas extracted from them) from three of the four discussion threads above to be potential keyword possibilities: digital printer for rapid prototyping; high quality prints on a used color digital printer; color press on textured stocks.

Many forums are subdivided into a long list of niche markets. Print Planet, for example, included forums specifically for prepress and workflow, post press and binding, ink and substrates, wide format, etc. Each niche within the niche included a ton of threads likely to be ideal for mining ideas.

Just start typing in Google

Google and other search engines attempt to anticipate your search needs based on user history. As you see here, "home remodeling" invoked a trio of related ideas.

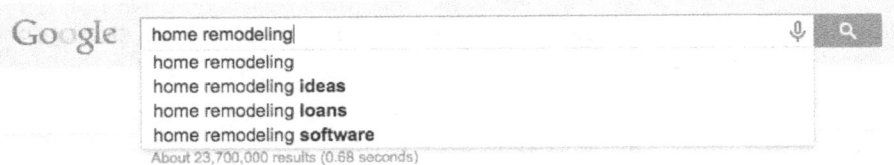

Bing was even more prolific.

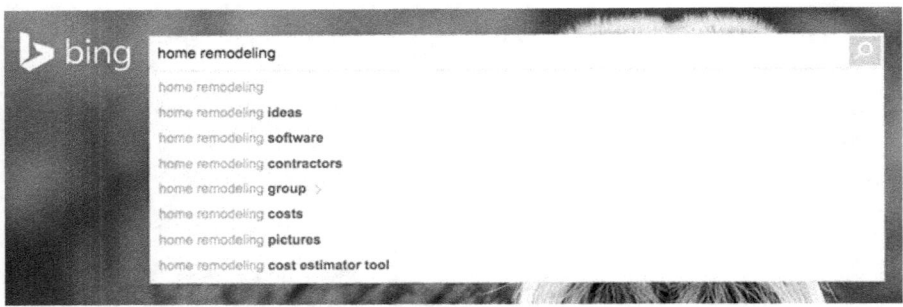

After performing your search, be sure to scroll to the bottom of the page where you'll find an additional, usually longer, list of suggested keyword strings. Some are related ideas, but don't include the exact words entered, such as "bathroom" and "additions."

eHow is a keyword epicenter

eHow, a popular site from Demand Media, can be a keywords goldmine. The website attempts to find long tail keywords it can rank for with highly targeted content. I put myself in the mindset of a massage therapist and simply searched "massage." The following is a small sample from the many pages served.

How to Use Pressure Points for a Foot **Massage**
How to Use Pressure Points for a Foot **Massage**. A foot **massage** can do great things for your feet and other parts of your body. Feet have pressure points that ...
http://www.ehow.com/how_2331049_use-pressure-points-foot-massage.html

How to Make Natural **Massage** Gel
How to Make Natural **Massage** Gel. Because they don't flow, **massage** gels are easier to work with and less messy than oils. Unfortunately, while there are ...
http://www.ehow.com/how_5623080_make-natural-massage-gel.html

How to Heat Stones for **Massage**
How to Heat Stones for **Massage**. **Massage** is a therapeutic, relaxing and delightful way to release tension and maintain health. There are so many different ...
http://www.ehow.com/how_6939143_heat-stones-massage.html

You might say, "Yeah, but with the might and technology behind the eHow site, I'll lose the battle to them." Perhaps not. In a helpful eBook from Wordstream, *How to Find Your Most Cost-Effective Keywords*,[4] the author explains the content tends to be produced on the cheap and therefore, is often lame. Considering the many changes Google has made in recent years to favor deep and informative content, it's possible, even with minimal domain or page authority, you can create superior content to rank on the first page.

Try Q&A sites

The keyword hunting strategy I explained above where you tap into forums can also be applied on question and answer websites including:

- Quora (https://www.quora.com/)
- Yahoo Answers (https://answers.yahoo.com/)
- Answers.com (http://www.answers.com/)
- Askville by Amazon (http://askville.amazon.com/Index.do)

On Quora, I searched for "Facebook advertising" and found questions about "advertising mobile apps" and "ways to track conversions" among a very long list of questions. The answers too, provide helpful hints. For instance, the first answer for the first question below included "promoting app downloads" and "algorithms for the optimization of ad programs."

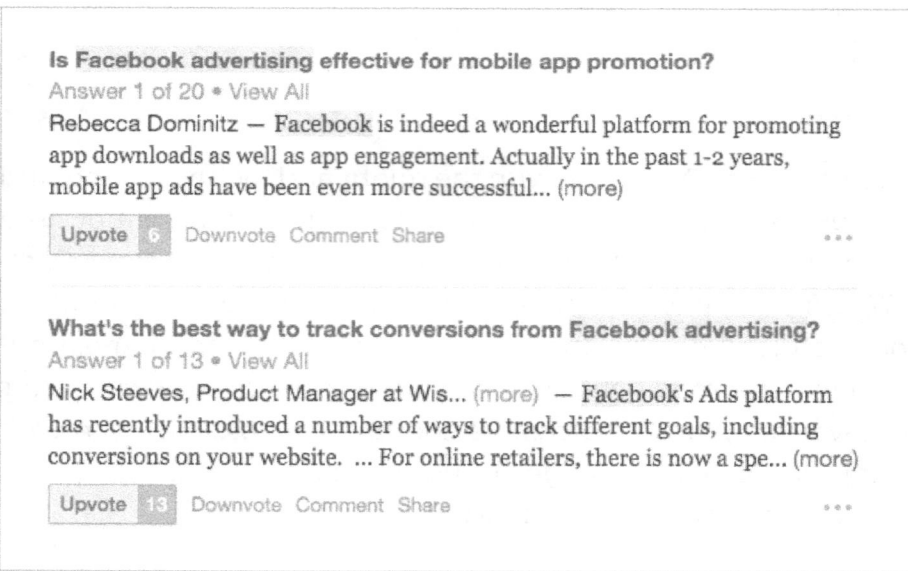

If you like this strategy, check out these tips for using Quora as an SEO idea source.[5]

Free and fabulous keyword suggestion tools

Ubersuggest.org and Keyword-tool.io are two free tools that suggest massive lists of keywords for just about any term you enter. I tried "bifocals."

↥ **bifocals + f**

- bifocals facts
- bifocals for shooting
- bifocals for astigmatism
- bifocals for sale
- bifocals franklin
- bifocals for child
- bifocals for handgun shooting
- bifocals for reading only
- bifocals for reading
- bifocals for pilots

The list here is for keywords where bifocals is followed by an "f." The keyword suggestions tools cover the entire alphabet. You can click any phrase to invoke even more. I clicked the plus sign for the first one above and got "bifocals fun facts" and more.

Happy hunting

If you take just one idea away from this chapter, let is be this: long tail dominates Google search activity and every form of search. In fact, CNET reported[6] 15% of Google queries have *never* been seen before. That's 75,000,000 searches per day.

Armed with an understanding of this reality, take a smart approach by finding niche keywords. Dig deep aiming to uncover real world jargon. Try some or all of the six approaches I've suggested. Identify long tail keywords to inform your content development and seize a competitive advantage.

CHAPTER 4

OFF-PAGE, LOCAL AND VIDEO SEO

Off-page SEO

Off-page SEO encompasses the tactics used to increase the authority of your site, increase visibility via search engine rankings, and drive traffic. Much of the emphasis in off-page SEO is link acquisition, or, link building. By earning external links to your web pages you signal to the search engines the pages offer valuable content.

For years, optimizers used a variety of tactics that have been rendered worthless by a series of changes to the algorithms used by the search engines. Today, such tactics are dubbed "black hat" and are recognized by Google and other search engines. Besides being taboo, black hat SEO methods are actually detrimental to the cause.

Success in link building now comes from earning natural links from legitimate sites. While the quantity of links is a ranking factor, even more important is the quality of the links. A natural link means the website owner purposely included a link to your page, most likely because they like something written or published on it.

While there are a variety of ways you might earn backlinks, the two best ways are creating guest posts for respectable blogs and publishing great content on your website and blog. To succeed with SEO, you must focus on both on-page and off-page SEO.

It's important to understand, off-page SEO is an ongoing process and will seldom produce results quickly. Your efforts in content marketing and social media marketing must be ongoing to be productive for earning backlinks.

Local SEO

Local SEO is critical to location-based businesses, but commonly ignored and largely misunderstood. Conversion rates tend to be high for companies who succeed with local SEO because the potential customer is likely to be looking to satisfy an immediate need.

For obvious reasons, the growth of local SEO is fueled by the immense popularity of mobile devices. Simply put, the smartphone search has replaced the yellow pages. When you make local SEO work for your business, you generate traffic online and physically. When you don't, you're essentially invisible to the online shopper.

Successfully integrating local SEO calls for numerous strategies including:

- An optimized listing on Google My Business (formerly Google Places)

- Website pages featuring geo-targeted titles and relevant content
- Submitting and verifying name, address and phone information to local business directories such as Yelp, Citysearch, MerchantCircle, etc.
- Getting reviews
- Citations in local directories
- Involvement on local blogs

Video SEO

Google, which owns YouTube, loves video. At one point, research by Forrester indicated you're 50 times more likely to appear on the first page of search when your page features a video. Because videos are presented with "rich" snippets, that is, they include thumbnail images, they also command ultra-high click-through rates.

Clearly, your SEO efforts are amplified when you optimize your video pages. However, the search engine does NOT extract information from the video itself when it crawls and indexes a page. You need to optimize the page containing the video, which may include:

- The use of a video site map
- Populating the title tag properly
- Publishing a transcript of the video or listing its highlights
- Making your video embeddable on other sites

CHAPTER 5

HOW TO AVOID SEO B.S.

We're up to our earballs in misinformation about SEO. There is BS everywhere.

SEO BS is on your screen. Ironically, if you do a search about search, your search engine will help you find tons of it. Even the shysters can optimize a few pages.

SEO BS is on your bookshelf. This is an unavoidable problem. You could have bought books from honest and legit authors who are SEO experts. If the book's a few years old, much of its content probably stinks now.

SEO BS is in your inbox. Not true? I'm happy to share mine. I get email, contact form spammers, and LinkedIn messages nearly every day from some "expert" who promises to quickly propel my site to the first page of search. I always wonder: if the sender is so good at SEO, why the need to send spam? Wouldn't the many companies in need of their services find them?

We have the BS-SEOs to thank

The reality is SEO doesn't have rules. We look to experts like Moz for helpful guidelines, research, and case studies. Their lessons are helpful. *Sometimes.*

People that do SEO tend to call themselves SEOs. They want us to believe they're professional optimizers. Some are. I respect these people—the digital marketers who specialize in search— immensely.

But it can be challenging to quickly spot who's full of it and who's not. The first and most important test is to look for guarantees. Guarantees are BS.

Real SEO pros can guarantee to work diligently on your behalf to generate qualified leads via search. That's all they guarantee. BS SEOs tend to guarantee rankings.

I don't want you to buy their bull. Ask yourself these questions before buying into any SEO service agreement.

- **Will the SEO company audit your website?** This is a necessary first step. Companies that want to jump right into getting you links are reckless.
- **Are you being promised high rankings?** Run for it. One, this is not a trustworthy promise. Two, SEO is marketing. High or otherwise, rankings only matter if they drive qualified prospects to your website and help achieve your marketing goals.
- **Will the SEO company school you?** How much you want to understand and be involved in SEO is up to you, but what they're doing should never be a mystery.
- **What will you get?** The answer needs to be reports, insights and action plans based on them. SEO is an ongoing process. Don't buy campaigns, any sort of backlinks blitz or x-thousand hits on your site.

B.S. detectors

Be on the lookout for the things the scammers say and do.

- Game the system—No one's going to admit to doing this, but that won't stop them from using black hat (unethical) tactics to get good short-term rankings. If you've paid any attention at all in recent years, you know Google has revamped their algorithm to not only detect the gamers, but also penalize them.
- High speed, volume link building—This is the gamer's stock in trade. They spam the web with links, duplicate articles, blog comments, and get you links on tons of worthless directories.
- Buying links—Red flag of the highest order. Real SEOs don't buy links. Some slime balls will tell you they don't have to because they own high value domains. Don't go there.
- Promises rankings—This one deserves a second mention. Don't be fooled into believing rankings are all you need.

SEO probably changed today

You simply need to accept this. You may not like having to concede the teams behind the search engines are working daily to tweak the algorithms, but if you're a content marketer, you probably should.

The search engine's goal is to reward the best content creators. Your goal should be to become one.

The unsolvable mystery all across the SEO universe is what factors affect your rankings. Experts will tell you the list may be as long as 200. But beware: if they go on to tell you how your use of a tactic *CAUSES* your rank to increase or decrease, they're not actually experts; they're liars.

The true experts steer clear of proclamations about causation because they know they can't deliver proof. Instead, they deliver data and insights about *correlation*.

I'll demonstrate by highlighting the hotly debated topic of "social signals." First, there should be no debate. Google said social signals are not a ranking factor. So for now, they're not. Note they did not say social signals will *never* be a ranking factor, right? They could, and likely will, change their tune.

Now, one of the most respected voices in SEO is Searchmetrics. Their 83-page white paper, SEO Ranking Factors and Rank Correlations 2014,[7] is one of the deepest studies on the topic I've seen.

The research says social signals is the area with the highest correlations to high rankings. "In other words, good ranking URLs have many shares, likes, comments, +1s and tweets," they wrote.

If you're not confused enough, I'll add that it's almost universally agreed that a high level of social media activity indirectly affects search rankings because it affects many of the factors that do affect rankings. But today, social signals are not a ranking factor. Okay?

I want to share some of the conclusions from the Searchmetrics report to help calibrate your BS detector and not be misinformed about false or old information about ranking factors.

Ranking correlations you want to know

Searchmetrics reports:

- The days of keyword density are over.
- High quality, relevant content is the focus of search. It is identifiable by higher word-count and semantically comprehensive wording. It's often enriched by images and video.
- To further understand the point above, realize Google recognizes "content clusters," which means variations of the keywords that are developed naturally in the copy.
- Keywords remain vital, but the trend is moving away from a single keyword towards entire topics.

- The quantity and quality of backlinks remains crucial.
- Search results vary and are influenced by personal search history.
- Search engines do not favor pages that meet certain technical on-page criteria (load speed, length of URLs, position of keyword in title, etc.). However, the absence of these criteria has a negative effect on ranking.
- Pages in top search positions have comparatively more internal links than those further down the rankings.
- More advertising integrations correlates to lower rankings.
- Backlink quality factors are probably the most important SEO metric on the "off-page" side.
- Correlated for search results, click-through rate is *the highest ranking factor.*
- User signals including time on-site and bounce rates are strong quality signals.
- SERPs for mobile are different.
- A good search position cannot simply be achieved by ticking a few of these boxes. Search engine assessment is multifaceted.

All you can do is listen, learn and experiment

I didn't mean to confuse you. Observations, reports, and opinions about SEO are bound to be forever conflicting. Again, the most timeless tip is to create useful content. It's the one piece of advice that will never be BS.

I recommend you learn enough to recognize crap advice when you hear it and steer clear of the BS artists. And finally, recognize the way SEO works changes constantly.

CHAPTER 6

PAY-PER-CLICK IS THE FAST WAY TO PAGE ONE

In this chapter, I want to usher you outside of the world of organic search or SEO and discuss another subset of search engine marketing (SEM) called pay-per-click (PPC). You'll find the term often referred to as AdWords. This is Google's PPC program, which is the pioneer of the industry and the leader by far.

You need to understand if you don't have the luxury of writing for one of the web's most established websites, search engine optimization (SEO) is *the hard way* to rank on page one. Gaining visibility and generating leads requires creating stellar content and a ton of persistence. It's not magic. And there are no shortcuts.

Pay-per-click (PPC) is a different story. Patience is not required. You can enjoy results immediately.

You won't succeed with zero understanding of the AdWords PPC advertising platform, however this chapter will give you enough knowledge to get started and put you on the path to success.

PPC is a money game

With pay-per-click, you get your web page displayed on the search engine results page (SERP) when someone searches for the keywords you've selected. As the name suggest, you pay only when your ads are clicked. Fees are based on a cost-per-click.

Less clicks, more conversion

It's no secret: far more searchers click on organic results than paid. However, PPC ads appeal to people that are shopping, hence they perform better for sales.

MarketLive claims paid search visits have a 35% higher conversion rate for e-commerce websites compared with visits from organic search (as reported by MarketingProfs[8]). Visitors arriving from paid search links had a 2.6% average conversion rate in the first six months of 2013, compared with a 1.9% conversion rate for organic search visits.

3 keys to AdWords

Paid search campaigns rely on three elements: keywords, ad creation, and landing pages. The effective PPC advertiser optimizes each of them.

1. Keywords—You create a list of keywords that will invoke the display of your ads when people search for them.
2. Ad creation—You create ads to be shown when the keywords are searched. The goal, of course, is to make them relevant and compelling so they earn the click.

3. Landing pages—When viewers click on an ad they arrive at your landing page. The objective of your landing page is to earn a conversion, which can be a variety of actions such as purchasing, downloading, enrolling, etc.

What determines the costs?

Your per-click cost is determined by (1) your bid and (2) quality score.

Click fees are determined by an auction format. Your head might spin if you insist on knowing exactly how it works. In this chapter, I'll offer a passage from an AdWords help page[9] and then move on:

> Every time someone searches on Google, AdWords runs an auction to determine the ads that show on the search results page, and their rank on the page.

Google explains that to place a bid in the auction, you first choose *how* you'd like to bid. Your bidding strategy can focus on getting clicks, impressions, or conversions. The majority of AdWords programs use the clicks strategy.

Quality score is an algorithm that scores ads for relevancy to determine how closely the ad's keyword relates to the content of its associated landing page.

Yes, Google crawls your landing pages. Their job is to make sure users land on relevant pages. Quality score keeps advertisers in check and makes the game fair.

Thanks to the quality scoring system, your ad may be displayed before others that bid higher because it is deemed more relevant. As such, quality score helps determine the cost-efficiency of your keywords, which in turn, helps optimize your choice of keywords.

In a successful PPC campaign, you'll create a strong relationship between your keywords, ad copy and landing page.

Match-making

AdWords offers three match types for keywords: exact match, phrase match, and broad match. Google offers a help page that defines each match type in detail.[10]

You might apply multiple strategies for setting match types. There is no correct or incorrect approach. Ultimately, your performance metrics will help guide your choices.

Exact match

- Targets more specific searches
- Limits your reach
- Increases the risk of missing-out on potential leads

Phrase match

- Broadens the parameters to include close variations of the exact phrase
- May include misspellings

Broad match

- Increases traffic (but doesn't ensure it's qualified traffic)
- Creates the need to closely monitor which search queries are coming through
- Enables the use of negative keywords to reduce poor matches

When launching new campaigns, consider using broad match and phrase match to maximize clicks. After a while, pull reports to identify the keywords that converted best and set them to exact match.

Your keyword choices and match types will change. You'll experiment, examine and refine on an ongoing basis.

For greater efficiency, Google AdWords accounts should be structured as campaigns containing ad groups. Use your ad groups and campaigns to stay organized.

Setting your AdWords budget

To manage your spend, you can set a daily budget at the campaign level. You're free to assign specific budgets per campaign and change it when you like.

You'll be presented various options to allocate your dollars over time. For example, you can allow your budget to be used each day until it's depleted or spread out throughout the day.

Beginning advertisers are wise to start small, setting a low budget initially.

You'll quickly get insights regarding lead quality and can boost your budget if you're pleased with the results.

Remember, you pay per click, so it's conceivable your daily budget won't be spent every day. It's only when your ads are working (that is, getting clicks) that you'll see your charges reaching the levels you set.

Let's examine how to make your ads work.

Compel searchers to click

Given the PPC model, the goal is reach your maximum spend each day because you're getting the clicks you want. Here's where the writing of your ads comes into the picture.

There's not much to it. Literally. AdWords ads are concise. They're also inflexible and uniform. You play by the following rules.

■ Headline—Your headline (or title) can have up to 25 characters. It will be displayed in blue in a slightly larger font than the remaining lines.

■ Display URL—A URL with a 37-character limit is displayed on the following line. Your display URL may be your home page, however, the actual page (destination URL) you direct readers to can (and should) differ. It can be any length.

■ Description lines—Two description lines, limited to 35 characters each, follow. The second description line is commonly used as a call to action.

The guidelines above apply to the typical format of a paid search ad, which appear in a sidebar on the SERP. For popular categories, ads often appear atop the page (and even the bottom) and in this case, they are organized slightly differently.

11 tips to optimize AdWords conversion

1. Use your keywords—Include your keywords at least once. Consider placing keywords in the headline and descriptions. They will appear bolded when they match the search inquiry.

2. Be clear—AdWords doesn't accommodate creative writing. Get right to the point.

3. Call for action—Write a short, focused, actionable call to action featuring verbs such as: get, save, shop. Suggest urgency, when appropriate with phrases such as: limited time, today, now.

4. Offer a benefit—Compel action by appealing to the reader's psyche with a benefit statement. A post from Unbounce[11] says to "mirror the visitor's end goal."

5. Differentiate—Read your competitors' ads in an effort to identify a unique selling proposition for yours.

6. Localize—Create geographically specific ads.

7. WIIFM—Answer "what's in it for me?" by addressing pain points and desires.

8. Be specific—Be as specific as possible about your solution. Note that specific does not mean sensational. Watch the superlatives. Stay credible.

9. Get it right—Let no mistakes slip by. Check your spelling and grammar.

10. Abide by the rules—AdWords enforces rules prohibiting symbols and capitalization. (See end notes for a resource regarding AdWords rules.[12])

11. Review your work—Always preview your ads before submitting them. Look to remove redundancies and format the ad as elegantly as possible.

The bonus tip: ad extensions

Google allows you to include ad extensions, which feature additional links. They'll appear in blue type, below your description lines. Take advantage of ad extensions by including information on offers, locations, additional landing pages and even phone numbers.

Extensions will increase the real estate you get and deliver additional information the reader may find helpful. There's no charge for extensions, so try them.

Extensions may be created automatically or manually. You may also have some control to edit or remove extensions created by Google. (See end notes for a resource regarding how extensions work.[13])

---

130 Hotels in Seattle WA - Up to Half-Price on Hotels
🔲 www.booking.com/**Seattle-Hotels** ▾
4.6 ★★★★☆ rating for booking.com
Book your **Hotel** in **Seattle** WA.
Free Cancellation · 24/7 Customer Service · Read Real Guest Reviews
Featured: Hotel FIVE, 11th Avenue Inn Bed And Breakfast, Kings Inn...

   Best Price Guarantee   No Booking Fees
   Book Now   Secure Booking

This ad features a number of extensions (generated automatically by Google, as they often are.)

Measuring PPC success

The granddad of today's modern data-driven marketing has to be pay-per-click. PPC is inherently rich in metrics. That said, this section could expand into a separate book. Let's aim for the cliff notes here by examining the most essential metrics.

- Impression—An instance of your ad being served as a result of a search.
- Click—A viewer clicks on your ad.
- Conversion—The viewer clicked and then took action on your landing page. Tracking code is used to measure conversions.
- Spend—The amount of money spent to date, per account.

Useful analytics will be derived from the above metrics, which you'll use to optimize your campaign. These include:

- Click through rate (CTR)—The percentage of impressions that result in clicks.
- Conversion rate—The percentage of clicks resulting in conversions.
- Cost per click (CPC)—The amount spent on each click.
- Cost per acquisition (CPA)— The amount spent on each conversion.

Your goal is to perpetually increase efficiency as measured by the cost metrics. As you optimize your keywords, ads, and account structure, you'll measure campaign performance and work toward reaching your goals.

Increase AdWords performance with split-testing

AdWords offers a built-in split-testing feature, to help you optimize PPC ads based on actual performance. This means you'll have an A and B version that differ. They'll be served 50/50, giving you results to indicate a winner based on click-through rate and/or cost-per-click.

In a video published by QuickSprout,[14] Brian Dean of Backlinko explains the process.

- He recommends testing your title, the first line, the second line, and the display URL. Brian suggests you don't change your landing page when split-testing ads.
- One approach is to create completely different headlines, description lines and URLs.
- Another more pointed approach is to split-test ads against one another by changing a single variable. Your headline is an obvious candidate.
- You need a significant enough sample to validate your results.

Serious PPC advertisers work with pros

I told you it's not difficult to get started with PPC, but also warned it can get tricky and technical. If you're battling for highly competitive keywords and aiming to perpetually improve ROI, you'll benefit from enlisting the help of PPC pros.

Also, the Google AdWords program changes often, so though you know more now than you did ten minutes ago, it's always a challenge to keep up.

BONUS 1

HOW TO GET YOUR BLOG POST ON THE FIRST PAGE OF GOOGLE

In this interview, I'm speaking with my friend Andy Crestodina, author of Content Chemistry and strategic director and co-founder of Orbit Media Studios in Chicago.

Barry: In most of our conversations about content marketing we talk about how it flies alongside search and when you understand both you're much more likely to succeed in driving traffic to your website. So I thought today we'd talk about search and particularly how it relates to your blog.

Andy: Sounds good. Yeah, this is a favorite topic of ours.

Barry: *The topic today is,* ***"How to Get Your Blog Post on the First Page of Google."*** *It's an ambitious goal, but I think it's understood now that there really is no other page. What do you think about that?*

Andy: I think that's mostly true. I just saw a study. The click through rate of pages that rank on the second page of Google is something like 5 percent. Page three is even lower than that. So 90-plus percent of clicks in Google are happening on the first page. Something like 18-plus percent of those rank in the first position.

Barry: *Yeah, so I guess I'll share the joke since not everybody knows the joke, but it's a popular joke: the best place to hide a dead body is the second page of Google. I suppose it's not entirely true. The good news is 4% of the investigators will find your dead body there.*

Do you approach your blog post with the goal of ranking on the first page? Are you thinking far in advance, "I'm going to write about something and be on page one of Google"?

Andy: I do, definitely yes. I put in extra time, effort and energy into specifically finding key phrases and underlining pages with key phrases, and indicating relevance for those phrases—knowing that it's really my best, and only chance, of having content that gets discovered and read and shared and attracts an audience weeks and months and years after it goes live.

Email marketing and social media have very short half-lives so those are great sources of traffic, but in the long run I know if I write something and it's going to get read next month or next year that's just not going to happen unless I successfully ranked it by targeting a key phrase and indicating relevance.

Barry: *So are you one of the shady characters that allow the robots to come before the humans?*

Andy: No, I don't think that ever really works. So let's say that you are shady and you wrote something that ranks and it stinks. How does that really meet any of your goals? If a visitor finds it they're just not going to stay. They're not going to share it. It's not going to convince them to take any action. It doesn't really get you any results. Ranking for its own sake, it's really like a vanity metric. It really won't meet any of your goals in the long run.

I deliberately try to make it the best page on the Internet for the topic.

Barry: *Yeah, what you just said made me think of something that I say a lot: the goal isn't really to get somebody to your website. The goal is to get somebody to subscribe to it. Would you agree with that?*

Andy: Yes. Traffic multiplied by conversion equals success (Traffic x Conversion = Success).

You have to have visitors and then the visitors have to take an action. Or else it was worthless. Anything times zero is zero. So we want visitors to come to the site. That's the first number and then we need a percentage of those visitors to act—that's the second number.

So all the ranking and traffic in the world will do nothing for your business at all unless you also have a conversion rate. Some percentage of those visitors commented, shared, subscribed, linked to it, mentioned it, referred to it... something else happened just beyond the visit.

Barry: *All right, so we got that straight. We're not seedy black hat SEO hackers. Our hearts are in the right place. We have* *value to share. We're going to write a post because we're going to help people understand a topic. And we can't really do that if there are no people. So we want to merge the world of high value and high discovery. And we're going to do that by thinking ahead when we create a blog post.*

So, you said it begins with a discovery or research process. How's that work? How do you say, I'm going to go take my blog post to page one? What's the first part of that exercise?

Andy: We're going to ask ourselves three questions in this process.

The first one is: is anyone searching for this phrase? We need to find a phrase that people are actually looking for. There's no point in ranking for a phrase if no one's looking for it. We joke that it'd be easy to rank for a phrase like ambidextrous armadillo. I can make the only page on the Internet that includes those combination of words. I can rank number one with that phrase next week. It would do me no good because nobody's looking for it.

Question two is: do I have a chance of ranking for it?

Question three is: can I make the best page on the Internet for the topic?

If you answer yes to all three of those, it's a worthy cause. Two out of three, don't bother. So we need to really find the answers to those three questions.

The first two questions are about keyword research. The first is search volume. The second's competition.

Barry: *Let's step through them. Search volume competition: how do you find out what is? And what are you looking for?*

Andy: There's lot of keyword research tools out there, but the bread and butter for all of us is really Google Keyword Planner. It's a part of AdWords. It's a massive set of data, so you just have to log into AdWords using any Google account.

You don't have to be an AdWords subscriber, or user, or advertiser.

Then, in the keyword planner, you enter a key phrase and it will tell you how many people are searching for that phrase every month or an estimate. Then it will tell you up to 800 suggested phrases that are related. Google made this to help advertisers finds more phrases to advertise and bid on.

So that's the first thing we want to check: volume. Are people truly looking for it? There are problems with that number, but that number will at least tell us, "Yes, people are looking for it." Or, "No, it's fewer than 10 searches per month on average. There's no numbers showing."

I don't chase big numbers in there. I don't say, "Oh, this one has 60,000 people searching for it. I need to really try to target that phrase." I'm mostly using this as a way to just validate it is in fact a phrase that has some demand. I don't put tons of stock in that number.

Google is now paying a lot of attention to semantics and synonyms and grammatical forms and it's really a search engine of topics more than phrases these days. But the tool only lets us search for phrases, so there's lots of little ways in which that number is not super accurate. It's the "exact match" number (searchers used the exact phrase). It does not show synonyms or any semantic linking. So just for that reason I'm just kind of validating if people are looking for it or not.

Barry: *Is there an inverse relationship between the popularity of the search volume for your chosen phrase and your chances of succeeding with it?*

Andy: There is. That's the second question. Do we have a chance of ranking for it? And generally speaking, just as you said, the longer, more specific the phrase, the less competition there will be for it, and therefore, the greater your chance of ranking for it.

So the single words or the "head phrases," say Super Bowl tickets, or HDTV, or digital camera—just forget about it. You have no chance of ranking for these unless you're a super famous and authoritative website.

So I target lots of very long specific phrases, but surprisingly there is demand for them. I rank right now for "How does social media affect SEO?" That's a long phrase. It's a full sentence. But something like 60 people a month are searching for it. That's quite a few people. So it's often surprising.

Barry: *Okay, so that springboards into your second question: do I have a chance? This has to do with the competition, right?*

Andy: Right. The number one factor in Google for ranking has, is, was and will always be the authority of the page. In other words, we're talking about the link popularity of the page and the domain in general. Are other sites linking to it? Is it credible among other sites?

Sonia Simone (of Copyblogger) jokes that Google is like the mean girl in high school. You can get her to like you, but not directly. You've got to get all the other people to like you first and then she'll like you. That's how Google works. So if your site has credibility among other websites—as in backlinks or incoming links from other sites—then you have more authority and a better chance of ranking in general.

Your domain authority (DA) is just a proxy, from Moz, for Google's own metric called PageRank. See, Google doesn't share PageRank anymore, so just use domain authority.

You can look it up using Opensiteexplorer.org and it will give you a number from 1 to 100. So you may have a domain authority of 30 or of 60, whatever that might be.

Now here's the trick and this is what most people miss. If you learn one thing from this lesson, take this away. Target phrases for which the domain authority of the other high-ranking pages is in the same range as yours.

If the other sites have a domain authority in the 80s and 90s, you're going to need a site with a domain authority in the 80s and 90s, to successfully compete with them sites for that topic. If the other sites are in the 20s and 30s and 40s, you'll have a chance if you're in that range.

We joke that you don't want to enter the Indy 500 on a bicycle. You'll lose every time. But you might win the Tour de France. You've got a bicycle. You're going to win every marathon. So if your domain authority is in a certain range, let's say the 40s, don't target phrases for which the other high-ranking sites have a domain authority much higher. But go ahead and target anything in the range of the 40s or lower.

Barry: *To help everyone understand what that looks like we should now add the MozBar to our tool set. The MozBar is a free extension that you'll install with a popular browser, probably Chrome or Firefox. When you toggle it on, it will show you the domain authority from Moz of all the listings on the search engine results page.*

(We skip forward now to Andy clarifying the difference between domain authority and page authority.)

Andy: The bottom line is it's not about domain authority in the end. It's about the authority of the specific page, or "page authority." Google does not rank websites. They rank web pages.

Barry: *Your page authority—if the page doesn't exist yet—is going to be zero, right? The page authority is going to grow over time. I guess if Sonia is here to help us extend our metaphor, you need people talking about you, liking you. That's like passing notes, right? That's social sharing, and links, and so forth. So you have to work on it after you've published.*

Andy: That's the perfect way to say it. It's so true. You can't compare the page authority of a page that doesn't exist yet to the authority of the high ranking pages. So domain authority is kind of the next closest thing. I think it's just an easier way.

Remember, we're not going to micro-manage Google. Don't try too hard to do these things. Just follow best practices. There's a competition column in Google Keyword Planner. Ignore it. It shows you competition for AdWords. Just turn on the MozBar. Know your own domain authority and get a sense for whether or not you're in the general range.

Sometimes it's obvious even before you turn on the MozBar because you see all the high-ranking pages come from super famous websites and you're not a super famous website. Okay, so you need to find a smaller pond where you've got a chance of being the bigger fish.

Barry: *So let's say I have moderately low domain and/or page authority, somewhere in the 10 to 20 range. It brings up the idea of long tail search strategy, right? We've talked about it a little bit without pointing out exactly what it means. You think you could give a concise explanation of what long-tail means?*

Andy: Sure. You said it earlier, the longer and more specific the phrase, the lower the search volume and the less competition. So long tail would be like five, six, eight-word phrases.

Here's a trick, go to Keywordtool.io. It will scrape Google Suggest for you and give you all kinds of suggested key phrases. Some of them are very, very long. Those are phrases that someone's looking for or else it wouldn't appear in Google Suggest. And so try targeting one of those phrases. They're going to be eight and ten-word phrases sometimes. Great. Pick that phrase. There's some demand for it. It might be fewer than 10 searches per month but you'll start ranking. You will see a trickle of traffic from these.

Barry: *All right so you are bouncing between tools now because you're using a tool to do keyword research and then you're using a Moz tool, probably the MozBar, to see if you're entering the right race.*

Andy: That's right, it's a balance. It's a mix. If we're a very young site with low domain authority we might choose something that has very low search volume but we have to pick our battles in the beginning. We want to know that we can win for something.

Barry: *Yeah and I think it's cool to think of it as a step on a ladder because you're also going to be thinking long-term about your authority. So you need people at your website. And you need people sharing it. And you need all the things that come with creating content that people actually care about.*

Andy: SEO is slow. I can't think of a slower form of marketing. It takes a long time. It took me seven years to rank high for "Chicago Web Design."

Barry: *All right, now let's move on. You're at the stage now where you're writing a headline. If we're talking long tail, you know three to eight words of your headline already and go from there.*

So having talked about the strategy and understanding the competition and then moving forth to get your blog on page one, now you've got to write a blog post. What kind of suggestions can you toss at me, as the writer of the blog, so that I'm playing according to the search rules and I stand a chance?

Andy: Question one: is someone searching for it? Question two: do we have a chance of ranking for it?

Question three is, can I make the best page on the Internet for that topic? Can I really write something great? Is it worthy of ranking? Google has 2,000 math PhDs on staff. You're not going to trick them. You really have to make something great and deserving of rank or else, why bother?

As you write that great piece of content on the topic, focus on the reader. Be legit. Write something good.

Once you've done that go back and make sure that you indicated relevance. I always say this phrase. I think we should rename SEO "indicate relevance."

- Did you use the phrase in those most important places to tell Google that yes, your pages is relevant for this topic?
- Is it in the title? Is it in the header?
- Is it in the body? It should be in there at least a couple of times. Don't go over the top with keyword density
- Is it in the meta description?

Leave it at that.

Barry: *Yeah, the thing you said that I think people might respond to would be the keyword density.*

Andy: I don't think density is what people thought it was. The algorithm in Google has advanced so far beyond that. People used to be like, "Oh, I want to get exactly 4.5% keyword density." I say, "Calm down. You don't' have to worry about that." Make a great page on the topic.

Here's a trick though: use synonyms. If you search for a phrase in Google and in the search results and see other words and synonyms and different grammatical forms bolded, that's an indication Google has created a semantic link between the phrase you're targeting and other phrases.

So don't just use the specific phase four to six times or a certain percentage of density. Try to use different forms. Different related phrases. Phrases that complement it. Phrases that are in the family in that topic.

Barry: *Okay so now you've done it. You've written your piece. You hit publish. Does it always work? Does it work a lot? Is it a hit and miss type of thing?*

Andy: It isn't exact science. Google is the blackest black box in the universe. No one knows what's going on.

It works maybe half the time for me and I've been doing this for 15 years. You just go live with something you believe in and then see what works. If it didn't work then generally we can try to make the phrase more competitive in terms of authority by linking to it from other pages. I specifically build links in guest posts and other internal linking and do whatever I can by linking to it.

Barry: *Before you publish or after you publish? Or both?*

Andy: After you publish. I joke with people, it's like, "Oh, I was targeting that phrase. If it didn't work I've got to keep working on that." When I say, "I have to keep working on that," that's what I mean. I have to write guest posts on related topics and link back to this page that I'm trying to optimize.

Barry: *How else might you optimize the already optimized and published page? You are not on page one, but you're ranked. You're on page two or three. It ain't over, right? You have a plan and you started into it with creating links. What else can you do?*

Andy: You can better indicate relevance by making the page more focused on the topic. You can do whatever you can to try to make the page higher quality. Simply improve the page. Make it longer. Make it more specific. Add a video. Add graphics.

Ultimately we're not going to try to reverse engineer Google as much as we are trying to collaborate with Google to help visitors discover quality. Help them surface great content, so they get better content. That's advice SEOs don't say enough, "Hey, your pages don't rank yet? Make it better. Go improve it."

Another thing is keep sharing it. Make it more visible. Put it into roundup posts. Get it into heavy rotation on social. See if some other people will maybe just discover it, mention it, link to it. That will help. But basically you want to either make it a better page or make it a more visible page among people who create links and might link to it.

Barry: SEO is complicated. It's even kind of a complicated term, you know?

Andy: It freaks people out. Things about it just turn people off immediately. I think what they miss—and I like this message coming from you because you are extremely credible on the topic—is quality is kind of understated in SEO. There's so much emphasis placed on tactics, tricks, and what are the SEO hacks out there. That's why I said question three is: can you make a great page on the topic?

Barry: I think Google's been around for a couple of decades and the first decade it didn't have what it takes to make an assessment about quality.

Andy: Right. And now they know. This is another clue and it's something that's hard for people to study. When I look at my site and I see the blog posts that get the most search traffic they're also the blog posts that people spend the most time reading. Five minutes on this page. Six minutes on this page. Four minutes here.

If people spend seven minutes reading, on average, it's because that page is high quality and quality is what correlates with rank. So don't try to reverse engineer Google. Just try to do something great.

Google's a research engine. Who's winning in Google? Wikipedia. Why? Because they made the best page on the internet for millions of topics. Go deep. Choose a big topic—a topic worthy of a serious piece of reference material.

8 REASONS YOU'RE NOT RANKING IN SEARCH RESULTS

Contributed by Jayson DeMers of AudienceBloom

Search rankings are tricky. You can be ranking very well one day, and then just when you think you've cracked the Google code, your rankings plummet.

Or maybe your pages have *never* ranked well in the search engines. Maybe you've optimized your website the best you know how, but you're still not ranking for your desired keywords, or any keywords at all.

Whether you've experienced a sudden drop in traffic or simply never managed to get your pages ranking in the first place, the passages that follow should help you identify or diagnose the problems.

1. Your site is new

I can't tell you how many times someone has said to me, "My site has been up for a month and it's still not ranking in the search engines!" Getting ranked for specific keywords often takes months. After 2-3 weeks, your site should be indexed by Google's, but by no means does this mean your pages are guaranteed high rankings.

To confirm your site has been indexed, go to Google and type in site:yoursite.com. You'll be shown all the indexed pages on your domain.

If no search results are returned, your site hasn't yet been indexed. While Google usually finds your site on its own, you can also sub-mit your site manually[15] just to be sure. Generally this is unnecessary. Google will find your site as long as it is linked to elsewhere on the Web, such as articles published on external publications, local directories, or even tweets posted on Twitter that include a link to your website.

2. You're targeting high-volume keywords

Just 5 years ago, targeting short, high-volume keywords was the norm. Webmasters would create content based on these desired words or phrases, build some keyword-rich links back to their website, and watch their site climb the rankings for the keywords.

However, over the past few years, this strategy has become ineffective due to a collision of factors. Google released its Penguin algorithm[16] in April 2012, which specifically targeted and penalized websites with too many keyword-rich inbound links, since they are almost certainly unnaturally acquired, which is a violation of Google's webmaster guidelines.[17] Additionally, with so many sites vying for high-volume keywords, your chances of ranking anywhere close to the top are practically zero.

The truth is, ranking for popular seed keywords has become far less desirable. Short keywords will drive general traffic, whereas longer, more specific keywords will drive more focused, targeted traffic. Ranking for long tail keyword phrases will not only be easier, it will often result in much higher conversion rates.

3. Your content sucks

"Thin" content is described as content that adds little value for readers. It's generally published by webmasters who have read or heard that publishing content to their website is important, so they publish content for the sake of publishing content without much regard for its quality or value.

Google's Panda algorithm,[18] first released in February 2011, was aimed at enforcing higher quality search results by penalizing Websites that published too much "thin" content.

There are two types of "thin" content: the kind of flimsy, low-value content that can result in a manual action against your site, and the type that—while not penalty worthy—simply offers no value to your website visitors. While you may not receive a manual penalty for the latter, it very likely won't be receiving much search traffic, buzz, shares, mentions, or inbound links from other authors. Even worse, if your content sucks, that reflects poorly on anyone who does happen across it, which could kill your conversion rates.

4. You've inadvertently blocked Google from accessing your site

There are a number of ways you could have unintentionally blocked Google from crawling and indexing your site. The most common is through an error in your robots.txt file.

This issue most often occurs after launching a new site, or after having moved your site from one domain to another. To ensure Google has full access to your site, go into your robots.txt file and take a look around. See something like this?

User-agent: *

Disallow: /

This indicates you have blocked Google from accessing your entire site. Fortunately, removing this code from the file should rectify the situation. You should see your rankings return to normal in a matter of days or weeks.

5. You aren't using proper on-page SEO

While SEO has undergone significant changes over the past few years, on-page optimization has changed very little. While the types of keywords you'll be targeting will be different (long tail, more specific phrases), the way you'll use them in your content remains much the same:

- Static, keyword-rich URLs
- Optimized title tags, headings and alt image tags
- Throughout your content, naturally, along with related keywords and phrases

You'll also want to make sure you're using appropriate topical targeting; meaning rather than focusing on one or two main keywords, you're crafting your content to cover a broader topic or theme. Not only will this strategy likely increase your rankings for each keyword, it will provide a better user experience and will naturally attract more inbound links because the content will, in effect, provide more comprehensive coverage about the subject.

6. You don't have enough inbound links and mentions

A healthy inbound link profile is extremely important for getting your pages to rank high in search engines. What do I mean by "healthy?"

- Natural links from high-quality, authoritative, relevant sites
- A sufficient number of non-linked brand mentions
- Appropriate relationships between sites via co-citations
- A sufficient number and quality of deep links (links not just to your homepage, but to internal pages)

7. You haven't built trust with Google

Due to the release of the Penguin algorithm in April of 2012, online marketers have focused heavily on avoiding "over-optimization" of links. Since the release, Google has come down harder on sites that attempt to game the system by manually and manipulatively building keyword-rich links to a particular piece of content.

While over-optimization is certainly something that should be avoided, Brian Dean at Backlinko has presented some solid evidence[19] that sites with over-optimized anchor text can avoid being penalized *if they have built up a sufficient level of trust with Google*. In other words, Google may just forgive over-optimization, if it happens within the context of an otherwise trustworthy site.

8. Your site has been hit with a manual or algorithmic penalty

A key characteristic of an algorithmic penalty is a severe and sudden drop in rankings and organic search traffic. If you've been slapped with a manual penalty by Google, you'll likely experience a similar drop in rankings and traffic, along with receipt of a manual action notification via your Google Search Console account.

An algorithmic penalty will usually be harder to identify. Because Google is updating their algorithm on a regular basis, it can be difficult to correlate a drop in traffic with an update. However, if you can identify a specific date on which your rankings fell, you can try matching it up to known updates. Moz's Google Algorithm Change History[20] can help with this. Knowing which update caused your drop in rankings will allow you to fix the specific problems that caused the loss in the first place.

For help with recovering from manual penalties, see The Definitive Guide to Google Manual Actions and Penalties[21] and for algorithmic penalties, see Your Guide to Common SEO Penalties and How to Recover from Them.[22]

BONUS 3

15 SEO COPYWRITING TIPS TO DRIVE TRAFFIC TO YOUR SITE

Contributed by Brian Dean of Backlinko

Knowing SEO is great. Knowing copywriting is great. But when you can do BOTH? That's when you can slap a big ol' "S" on your chest because you'll be unstoppable.

And today I have something that will make you feel like you have SEO superpowers: 15 insanely actionable SEO copywriting techniques that you can use right now.

1. Use Udemy to Make Your Content 2-3x More Compelling

Most people think SEO copywriting is all about *putting words after words*. But in my experience, the STRUCTURE of your content is just as important as the writing itself.

And what better place to find proven content structures than Udemy? (Udemy is a MASSIVE directory of online courses.)

First, head over to Udemy and enter a keyword. For example, let's say you were writing a blog post about photography. You'd search for "photography." Udemy will show you all of their popular photography courses.

Next, pick a course with a lot of reviews. Once you pick a course, take a look at how many people have already enrolled in it. *(Brian chooses the EasyDSLR course, with nearly 6,000 people enrolled.)*

Do you see how huge this is? You're looking at content that **6,000 people have shelled out cold hard cash to get access to.** That means you don't need to rely on your Spidey sense. You KNOW there's going to be demand for your content. Thousands of people have already voted—with their wallets.

Once you've found a popular course, scroll down to the "Curriculum" section. That's where you'll find the proven structure you can use for your next post. Obviously, you don't want to rip off the instructor's course. But you can use bits and pieces of the curriculum for your outline.

2. Add These Words to Your Content (And Make Google Happy)

Today's super-smart Google doesn't care how many times you cram a keyword into your article. Instead, it pays close attention to Latent Semantic Indexing[23] (LSI) keywords. (LSI keywords are a fancy way of saying, "synonyms and closely related words.")

These LSI keywords help Google understand what your page is all about. For example, let's say you do a Google search for "cars." How does Google know whether you're searching for...?

■ Cars, the vehicle

■ *Cars,* the movie

■ The 1970s rock band (with awful hair)

■ The Canadian Aviation Regulations (CARs)

The answer? LSI keywords.

Let's say your keyword was "laptop repair." First, search for that keyword in Google. Then, scan the page for bold words and phrases that *aren't* your target keyword.

From the first page for "laptop repair" Google bolds words like "notebook," "computer repair" and "fix." Google bolds those terms because it considers them VERY similar to the keyword you just searched for. (In other words, LSI keywords.)

Finally, sprinkle these bold terms into your content.

3. Rank #1 in Google with this SEO Copywriting Secret

Bold promise? Definitely. But stay with me. What's the big secret I'm talking about?

Creating your own keywords.

I'll explain. If you search for your brand in Google, you probably rank #1.

You may not have thought about it, but your brand is a keyword, a keyword that you automatically rank #1 for. But why stop there?

You can generate boatloads of extra organic traffic when you also brand your techniques and strategies.

For example: You've probably heard about *The Skyscraper Technique*,[24] my 3-step strategy for getting more organic traffic to your site.

Because I branded my strategy "The Skyscraper Technique," I now have a pipeline of extra visitors coming to my site every day. In fact, according to Google Webmaster Tools, the keyword "Skyscraper Technique" gets 1,103 searches per month.

Because I rank #1, #2 AND #3 for that keyword, I get the lion's share of those 1,103 clicks.

Bottom line? Whenever you develop a unique strategy, tactic, or technique, make sure you slap a branded name on it. When you do, you'll get a bunch of extra organic search traffic.

4. Stalk Forums for the EXACT Words Your Readers Use
A while back I published a post called, *Why Google Hates Your Site (Hint: It Has Something to Do With TrustRank)*.[25]

With this post I decided to go after a keyword that my competitors wouldn't bother targeting, even though it gets a decent amount of searches.

What was the keyword? **"Google hates my site."**

Believe it or not, I didn't pull this keyword out of thin air. I chose this keyword because I saw A LOT of people in SEO forums saying things like this:

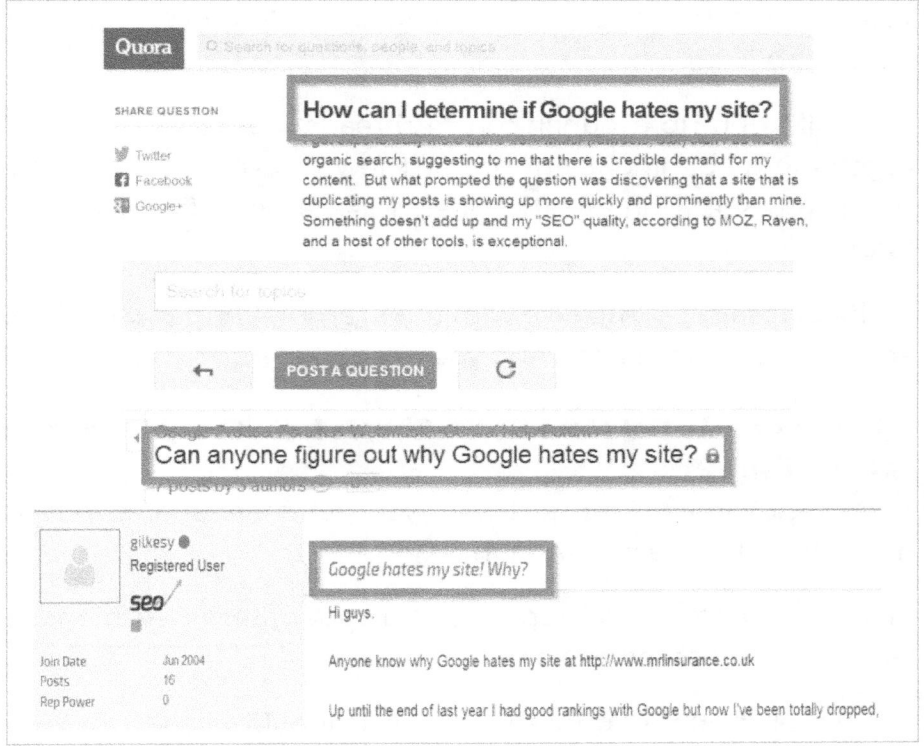

And if people post something in a forum, you can bet your butt that they also search for the same thing in Google.

So I decided to use a variation of that keyword in my post. Today, besides ranking #2 for my target keyword—TrustRank—when someone searches for "Google hates my site," I show up in the top spot.

How can you use this technique to get more traffic?

First, optimize your page just like you normally would. But before you hit "publish," scan forums for words and phrases people tend to use around your topic.

For example, let's say your target keyword was "organic vegetable gardening."

You'd search in Google with inurl:forum + "organic vegetable gardening."

This will bring up a bunch forum threads around the topic of vegetable gardening. Skim the first few threads that you find. When you see a phrase that seems like a good fit, search for forum + "phrase" in Google.

If a lot of results pop up (like with this example), add those words and phrases to your post. And you're good to go.

5. Here's How to Get More Social Shares from Everything that You Publish

Sure, social sharing buttons help you get more shares, but in most cases, they're not enough.

Instead, I recommend tapping into a copywriter's best friend: a call to action. Let me explain.

A few months back I published a post called *17 Insanely Action-able List Building Strategies That Will Generate More Subscrib-ers Today*.[26]

To maximize the amount of shares this post got, I included a "click to tweet" button underneath each item on the list. To date, my post has over 2600 tweets and a good chunk of those 2600 tweets came from my "click to tweet" buttons.

Here's how you can do the same thing. First, find a super action-able tip or strategy from your post. Next, head over to ClickTo-Tweet.com. Click on "basic link" and turn your actionable tip into a tweet.

Grab the link and pop the link into your post.

You can use buttons like I did. But plain-text links also work great. Whether you use a button or a plain link, definitely add at least one "click to tweet" call to action in your next post.

6. Here's How to Get More Search Engine Traffic... WITHOUT Higher Rankings

The higher you rank, the more clicks you get, *right*? Well...not really. I'll explain.

Right now Backlinko ranks #1 in Google for two different keywords: "how to do CPA marketing" and "how to find long tail keywords." (Obviously I rank #1 for more than just those two keywords. These are just two examples.)

Both keywords are "how-to" keywords. Both keywords have ads above the organic results. Yet the click through rate for "how to do CPA marketing" is 49% higher than "how to find long tail keywords."

Wait, what?

Here's the dead simple explanation: My Google listing for "how to do CPA marketing" looks WAY better than "how to find long tail keywords." It's got a clear title and compelling description copy.

On the other hand, my long tail keyword listing is a big mess. The title tag is cut off and the description tag is a random snippet from the page. Not good.

So follow these 2 simple steps:

First, make sure you write your own description tag for every important page on your site. If you don't, Google will sometimes write funky descriptions for you.

So pop open your SEO plugin of choice. Then, write a unique description tag for each important page on your site.

Next, tweak your title and description so that it *emphasizes the here and now.*

When someone does a Google search they want answers...FAST. And when you show them that you'll give them a quick win, you get more clicks.

For example, here's the Google result for my list building post:

17 Insanely Actionable List Building Strategies - Backlinko
backlinko.com/list-building
Learn how to quickly build your email list using these 17 insanely practical, proven strategies.

See how my title and description emphasize fast results not once, but twice? That's exactly what you want to do.

7. Hack Amazon to Get More Traffic to Ecommerce Product and Category Pages

With giants like Amazon littering the first page, it's not easy running an ecommerce site today. Despite that fact, I still see a lot of small ecommerce sites beat the odds. Their secret?

They target long tail keywords that most of their competitors don't know about.

Here's how they do it (and how you can do the same thing).

First, search for a product that you sell on Amazon.

For example, let's say you ran an ecommerce site that sold organic dog food. You'd search for "organic dog food" in Amazon. But don't hit enter!

If you wait a second, Amazon will show you long tail keywords related to that keyword (just like Google Suggest).

Grab one of those keywords and pop it into Google.

Check to see if the first page for the long tail keyword is less competitive than the one you're currently targeting. Usually, it will be. And because Amazon Suggest keywords are so laser-targeted, they tend to convert GREAT.

Finally, sprinkle those keywords into your product and category page copy (and in your title and description tags).

8. This Simple Strategy May Change The Way You Write Blog Posts

You probably already know that subheadings make your content MUCH easier to read. But what you may not know is that the copy that you use in your subheaders is a BIG deal.

You see, most people use random subheaders like "Building Links" and "Keywords." Sure, that breaks up the content, but random subheaders won't make a visitor say, "wow, there's a ton of value here."

Fortunately, there's a quick fix for that. Include benefits in your subheaders.

For example, in my post on building an email list, I include benefit-rich copy in most of my subheadings. Instead of a bland subheading like "Focus On Your Thank You Page," I put the BENEFIT front and center:

> ### 3. Optimize This Often-Ignored Page and Increase Your List By Up To 25%
>
> I've got good news and bad news...
>
> First, the bad news:
>
> If people double opt-in to join your list, up to 25% of your subscribers may be falling through the cracks.

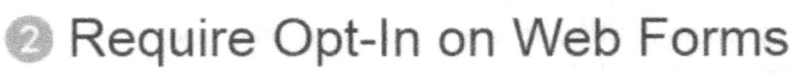

See the difference?

Include a benefit in AT LEAST 25% of the subheadings in your next post. When you do — BAM! — you'll instantly boost the perceived value of your content.

9. Gobble Up More Long Tail Traffic with "Title Tag Modifiers"

If you want more traffic from long tail keywords, the solution is simple: add "modifiers" to your title tag. What are "modifiers?"

Modifiers are words that you add to your title tags—words that get your site in front of more long tail searchers.

Here's little case study of this strategy in action:

A while back I published a guide called *Link Building: The Definitive Guide.*[27] The title tag I used was simply the name of the guide. At the time, I thought to myself, "This title tag is short and sweet. It also includes my target keyword. This is a great title tag."

But I was wrong. I quickly realized that I could get MORE traffic to that page if I added a modifier. So I added the keyword "SEO" to my title tag:

Link Building for SEO: The Definitive Guide

Thanks to that simple tweak, my page ranks for keywords that I wouldn't have thought to optimize around, like "SEO link building" (480 searches/month) and "link building SEO" (90 searches/month).

According to Google Webmaster Tools, those two keywords bring in 139 targeted visitors per month. All from (literally) 28 seconds of work.

How can you do the same thing? First, find a page on your site that has a short title tag (between 25-40 characters). Add a word or two to your title tag that you think your audience might use when they search for your target keyword:

If you're not sure what modifier to include, pick one from this list:

- "How to…"
- Review
- Checklist
- Guide
- Simple

You won't be able to predict *exactly* what keywords these modifiers bring in, but you'll get more search engine traffic than you would without them.

10. Skyrocket Time-on-Page With this Intro Formula

Backlinko rocks a very high average time-on-page of 4 minutes, 4 seconds (00:04:04).

I want to show you a technique that makes Google searchers stick to my site like superglue—one of my battle-tested blog post introduction templates: the APP Method. Here's what it looks like:

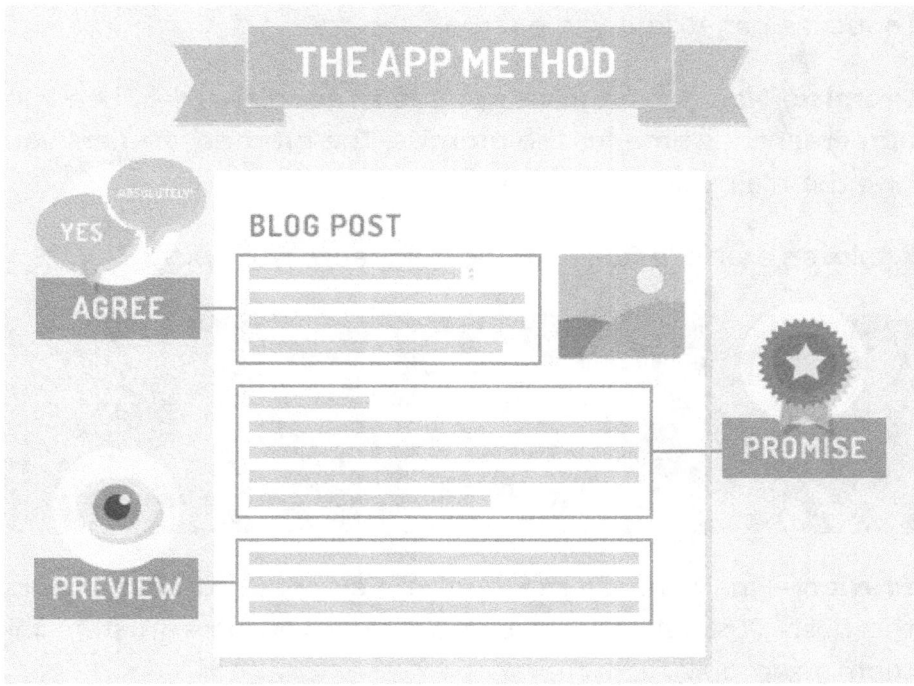

As you can see in the graphic, "APP" stands for: Agree, Promise, and Preview.

Let's break each element down:

Agree—Start your introduction off with an idea or concept that a Google searcher will agree with. This shows them that you understand their problem.

Here's an example from my post about creating a social squeeze page:

> I think you'll agree with me when I say:
>
> It's REALLY hard to convert ice-cold traffic into email subscribers.

That's something people searching for my target keyword ("squeeze page") know to be true.

Promise—Now that you've got them nodding their head in agreement, it's time for the promise. The promise is where you give them a peek into a better world.

Again, an example from the social squeeze page post:

> Well, it turns out, you can dramatically increase your site's email signups by adding one simple page to your site... a page that's converting 21.7% of my traffic into new email subscribers.

Preview—Finally, hit them with the preview. Don't beat around the bush. Just tell readers *exactly* what you have in store for them. Example:

And in today's post (and video) I'm going to show you what that page is... and exactly how you can easily add one to your site.

Once you put the finishing touches on the preview, you're set. You now have an intro that keeps Google readers on your site and a page that Google will want to show to more people.

11. Add More LSI Keywords with "Searched related to..."

Like I mentioned, the more LSI keywords you embed into your content, the better Google understands what your page is about. I've got a mini case study that will show you how to reveal even more LSI keywords that you can use.

A while back I wanted to add a few LSI keywords to my post, *On-Page SEO: Anatomy of a Perfectly Optimized Page.* First, I searched for my target keyword ("on page SEO") in Google.

Next, I scrolled to the bottom of the first page. This is where Google shows you "searches related to..." keywords. These are PERFECT LSI keywords to include in your content.

I grabbed any LSI keywords that made sense and popped them into my content. For example: *"on-page SEO checklist."*

And I was good to go. This technique has a bonus benefit too. "Searches related to..." keywords help you rank for long tail keywords that may not show up in the Google Keyword Planner. That means more traffic for you.

12. Borrow Headline Formulas from BuzzFeed and ViralNova

A lot of SEO and content marketers hate on "click bait" sites like BuzzFeed and ViralNova. Me? I think they're geniuses. Their meteoric growth speaks for itself. And they've proven that their headline formulas grab people by the eyeballs.

For example, I may have caught your eye with the subheader above: *This Simple Strategy May Change the Way You Write Blog Posts.*

The idea came from a post on BuzzFeed:

 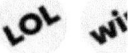

News   Buzz   Life   Entertainment   Quizzes   Videos

12 Things That Will Change The Way You See Color

Pimples look like "a multicolored Vesuvius" if you have extraordinary vision.

You can do the same thing. Just check out some recent posts on BuzzFeed and ViralNova and adapt them for your blog post titles and subheadings.

Obviously, some of their headlines are over the top. So I've put together a few BuzzFeed-style headline templates that grab attention...without going overboard:

- 25 ___ That Will Change The Way You ___
- I Tried ___ and Even I Was Surprised About What Happened Next
- This ___ Makes ___ 10x Better
- Here Are 11 ___ That ____. And They're Backed By Science
- Use These 20 Simple Hacks For More ____. #5 Is Awesome
- When You Learn About ___ You'll Never ____ Again

13. This Simple Strategy Stops "Serial Skimmers"

Everyone and their mom know that subheadings make online content easier to read. Subheadings are just ONE way to break up your content.

Magazines use dozens of different techniques to break up walls of text. And when you use the three magazine-inspired techniques I'm about to show you, you'll stop "serial skimmers" in their tracks.

1: Quote Boxes—Whenever you quote someone, put that quote in a box. Here's an example from Backlinko:

In Chris's words:

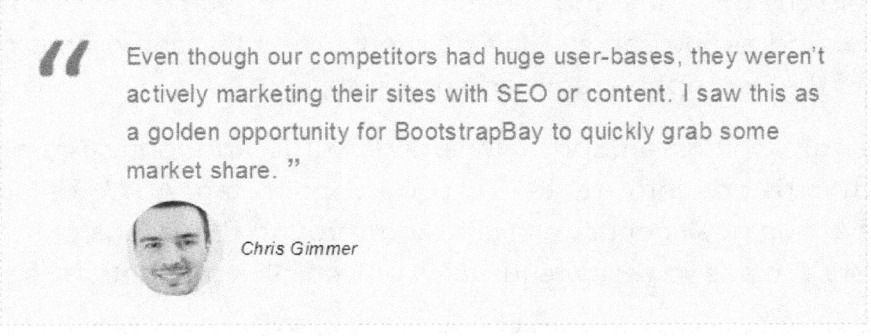

That's when he decided to try The Skyscraper Technique

2: Sidebar Callouts—This is another magazine staple. Whenever you have content that complements your post put it in a callout box. I use these quite a bit at Backlinko.

3: Section Banners—This technique is a bit more involved, but it'll make your content look super professional. Just add a custom banner underneath each subheading. You can get these custom banners made at a freelance site like Upwork (Upworkcom). Or, if you're in the mood for DIY, Canva (Canva.com) works well too.

14. Embed AdWords Copy to Get More Clicks to Your Organic Results

Now it's time to show you another proven strategy for attracting more clicks to your site. Let me show you how it works with a real life example. Here's what the listing for one of my posts used to look like:

> **17 Insanely Actionable List Building Strategies That Will ...**
> backlinko.com/list-building ▾
> Dec 23, 2014 - 17 insanely practical **list building** strategies that you can use to build your email list TODAY. Get More Email Subscribers: Click here to ...

Because I was in a rush to get this post out in time, I forgot to write my own title and description tag. So Google wrote it for me. And as you can see, it ain't pretty. The title tag was cut off and the description tag made no sense.

To turn things around, I included words and phrases from AdWords ads into my title and description tag. AdWords ads have one goal: generate clicks. And through thousands of split tests, the ads you see are (usually) proven click magnets.

For example, I noticed that most of the AdWords ads for the key-word "list building" had the words "email list" or "email lists." So I made sure to pop the phase "email list" into my description tag.

A lot of the AdWords ads I saw also used words like "build" and "grow." So I added the word "build" to my description tag too. And just like that I had a search result that's MUCH more likely to attract clicks.

15. Use This to Make Your Content More Compelling

You've probably heard of HARO (http://www.helpareporter.com), a service that connects journalists and sources. When a journalist needs a source for a story, he or she sends out a query. If you reply to a query with top-notch info, you can land mentions from some pretty baller sites.

But that's not what we're going to use HARO for today. Instead, we're going to use HARO queries to make our copywriting more compelling and attract more long tail traffic.

First, sign up as a source (it's free). Next, choose the HARO lists that fit your business. You'll start to get HARO emails from reporters and bloggers looking for sources.

Give each email a once over. Keep an eye out for any topics that you tend to cover on your blog. When you find one, pay attention to how the journalist phrases the topic.

9 times out of 10, the journalist chooses an angle because there's growing interest in that topic. In other words: people are searching for that topic in Google more and more.

So right off the bat you've got a great topic ("Cover Letter Best Practices") handed to you on silver platter. But don't stop there.

Pay close attention to the words and phrases the journalist uses in the query and make sure to include similar words and phrases in your content. And just like that you have a post built to gobble up more long tail traffic.

Now it's time to put these techniques into practice.

YOUR CHECKLIST OF SEO ESSENTIALS

The following checklist will help ensure your on-site SEO is solid.

- Install Google Analytics[28]
- Install Google Search Console[29] (formerly Google Webmaster Tools)
- Install Bing Webmaster Tools[30]
- If you're running on the WordPress CMS install All in One SEO Pack or Yoast SEO (https://yoast.com)
- Check Google Search Console for 404 and 500 errors, duplicate content, missing titles and other technical errors
- Used Browseo to find additional technical errors such as ineffective redirects (Browseo.net)
- Use Screaming Frog to find broken links and crawl problems (http://www.screamingfrog.co.uk/)
- Use Google's Keyword AdWords Keyword Planner and the techniques in this book to select keywords
- Try Ahrefs to look at competitor's link profiles (https://ahrefs.com/)

- Incorporate your primary keywords into your page URLs
- Make sure your title tags fit
- Write meta description tags
- Use your keywords in H1 tags
- Use keywords in your page copy (without overdoing it)
- Use synonyms or variations in your copy
- Use descriptive ALT tags and filenames for your images
- Create links to internal pages that both users and search engines can understand
- Make sure your site is free from duplicate content with canonical tags or use Google Search Console to fix any duplicate content
- Create an XML sitemap and submit it to Google and Bing Webmaster Tools
- Create a Robots.txt file and submit it in Google and Bing Webmaster Tools
- Check your site speed with Google Page Speed Tools[31]

END NOTES

1. Andy Crestodina, *Content Chemistry: An Illustrated Handbook for Content Marketing*, Orbit Media Studios, Inc.; Second Edition (September 15, 2014) http://www.orbitmedia.com/content-chemistry

2. Vanessa Fox, *Marketing in the Age of Google, Your Online Strategy is Your Business Strategy*, Wiley (Revised May 1, 2012) http://www.vanessafox.com/the-book

3. Brian Dean, *Keyword Research, The Definitive Guide*, Backlinko, http://backlinko.com/keyword-research

4. *How to Find the Most Cost-Effective Keywords*, A WordStream Guide (2013), http://www.wordstream.com/download/docs/longtail_keywords.pdf

5. Tom Demers, *Quora SEO: How to Use Quora if You're an SEO*, WordStream blog (March 24, 2011), http://www.wordstream.com/blog/ws/2011/03/24/quora-seo

6. Dan Farber, *Google Scratches its Brain 500 Million Times a Day*, CNET blog (May 13, 2013), http://www.cnet.com/news/google-search-scratches-its-brain-500-million-times-a-day

7. *SEO Rank Correlations and Ranking Factors—Google U.S.*, Searchmetrics, http://www.searchmetrics.com/knowledge-base/ranking-factors-2014/

8. Ayaz Nangi, *Paid Search vs. Organic Search: Which Converts Better?*, MarketingProfs blog (September 4, 2013), http://www.marketingprofs.com/charts/2013/11551/paid-search-drives-more-conversions-than-organic-search#ixzz3adnFgBG6

9. *AdWords Help*, Google, https://support.google.com/adwords/?hl=en#topic= 3119071

10. *Using Keyword Matching Options, AdWords Help*, Google, https://support. google.com/adwords/answer/2497836?hl=en

11. Johnathan Dane, *How to Write the Highest-Performing Google AdWords Ads, Ever*, Unbounce blog (February 9, 2015), http://unbounce.com/ppc/ write-high-performing-adwords-ads/

12. *AdWords Policies, AdWords Help*, Google, https://support.google.com/ adwordspolicy/answer/6008942?hl=en

13. *Enhance Your Ad with Extensions, AdWords Help*, Google, https://support. google.com/adwords/answer/2375499?hl=en

14. *How to Split Test Ads in Google AdWords* (video featuring Brian Dean), Quick Sprout, http://www.quicksprout.com/university/how-to-split-test-ads-in-google-adwords/

15. *Google Search Console, website URL submission page*, Google, https:// www.google.com/webmasters/tools/submit-url?pli=1

16. *Google Penguin*, Wikipedia (Last modified October 3, 2015), https://en.wikipedia.org/wiki/Google_Penguin

17. *Webmaster Guidelines*, Search Console Help, Google, https://support. google.com/webmasters/answer/35769?hl=en

18. *Google Panda*, Wikipedia (Last modified October 5, 2015), https://en.wikipedia.org/wiki/Google_Panda

19. Brian Dean, *Why Google Hates Your Site (Hint: It Has Something to Do with TrustRank)*, Backlinko, http://backlinko.com/google-trustrank

20. *Google Algorithm Change History*, Moz, https://moz.com/google-algorithm-change

21. Jayson DeMers, *The Definitive Guide To Google Manual Actions And Penalties*, Forbes.com (June 16, 2014), http://www.forbes.com/sites/jaysondemers/ 2014/06/16/the-definitive-guide-to-google-manual-actions-and-penalties

22. Jayson DeMers, *Your Guide to Common SEO Penalties and How to Recover From Them*, Huffington Post (Last updated: February 3, 2014), http://www.huffingtonpost.com/jayson-demers/your-guide-to-common-seo-_b_4378752.html

23. *Latent Semantic Indexing*, Wikipedia (Last modified October 22, 2015), https://en.wikipedia.org/wiki/Latent_semantic_indexing

24. Brian Dean, *Link Building Case Study: How I Increased My Search Traffic by 110% in 14 Days*, Backlinko blog *(Last updated August 20, 2015)*, http://backlinko.com/skyscraper-technique

25. Reference: footnote 19 above

26. Brian Dean, *17 Insanely Actionable List Building Strategies That Will Generate More Subscribers Today*, Backlinko blog (Last updated June 23, 2015), http://backlinko.com/list-building

27. Brian Dean, *Link Building: The Definitive Guide*, Backlinko, http://backlinko.com/link-building

28. *Google Analytics*, Google, https://www.google.com/analytics/

29. *What is Search Console?*, Google, https://support.google.com/webmasters/answer/4559176?hl=en

30. *Bing Webmaster Tools*, http://www.bing.com/toolbox/webmaster

31. *PageSpeed Tools*, Google, https://developers.google.com/speed/pagespeed/?hl=en

www.ingramcontent.com/pod-product-compliance
Lightning Source LLC
Chambersburg PA
CBHW070831180526
45168CB00002B/797